The Homing Pigeon

by The United States Army Signal Corps, War Department

NATAL PUBLISHING LLC

ARS LONGA, VITA BREVIS

U. S. GOVERNMENT PRINTING OFFICE
WASHINGTON: 1945

SECTION I

GENERAL

1. Purpose

This manual provides instructions for proper breeding, care, and training of the homing pigeon, and for the selection and training of enlisted pigeoneers. With certain modifications this information can be used by all pigeon units serving field forces, both in theaters of operations and in the zone of the interior. Instructions in FM 24-5 for units using the homing pigeon in communication have not been repeated. The mission, function, and operation of a signal pigeon company and the tactical employment of pigeons are described in FM 11-80.

2. Methods

The methods prescribed in this manual are based upon experience. Accordingly, if any new procedures are found by experience to improve pigeon communication they should be submitted to the Chief Signal Officer for consideration.

3. Origin and History

The homing pigeon used by the Army for signal communication (referred to in this manual as "pigeon," "homing pigeon," and "bird") is a distinct variety created through careful cross-breeding to obtain maximum distance and speed in controlled and directed flight. Homing pigeons are grouped in families or strains usually identified by the names of the civilian pigeon fanciers who bred them for many generations to develop certain characteristics of performance and appearance. When the several varieties of pigeons used to breed the modern homing pigeon actually originated is not certain. It is known, however, that the following varieties existed in England and Belgium before the nineteenth century, although the exact percentage and order of their blend have not been determined: Smerle, Horseman, Cumulet, Dragoon, Carrier, and Owl.

4. Nature

The principle of using homing pigeons as messengers is based on their instinctive attempt to return to their home lofts whenever they are removed some distance and released. They will do this even with an attached message or other light article. This desire to return is largely based on natural urges of hunger and reproduction. Because the pigeon has only one mate the reproductive urge is often the stronger. These impulses can be stimulated by CONTROLLED feeding, mating, and breeding without harming the pigeon's health.

5. Utility

The pigeon's usefulness to the Army is measured by the reliability and speed with which it returns to its loft. Speed and reliability are largely determined by the pigeon's strain, physical condition, training, and treatment. Therefore any lowering of standards for these factors will be a serious handicap. Further handicaps are discussed in E below. Section V sets minimum ability standards for properly-trained, well-bred, healthy birds to be used by combat units as message carriers.

A. Breeding. Since physical characteristics and homing instinct are usually inherited from the parents, records are maintained for each pigeon. Then pairs are selected, mated, and allowed to produce young birds on the basis of these records, plus other desirable attributes described in section VI.

B. Condition. The physical condition of a pigeon greatly affects its performance. Therefore, study physical characteristics of pigeons and enforce procedures prescribed in sections III and VII for feeding, watering, and maintaining proper physical condition.

C. Training. Training of the pigeon begins at an early age, and is progressive and constant. The object is to settle the pigeon in its home loft in order to develop reliability and speed as described in section V.

D. Treatment. The pigeon is highly sensitive and responsive to kindness, firmness, reward for good performance, and calmness of personnel handling it. Make the loft as attractive as possible because the pigeon prizes its home.

E. Handicaps. Bad weather, darkness, and injury, as well as inadequacies in breeding, conditioning, and training, reduce efficiency of pigeons (see **par. 9C**).

(1) BAD WEATHER. This includes snow, fog, rain, and adverse winds, or any other conditions which reduce visibility or oppose the flight of the pigeon. Generally, flights may be predicted according to certain atmospheric conditions as follows:

CONDITIONS	RESULTS
Blue sky, high ceiling with white fleecy clouds, and low humidity.	Very fast speed.
Solid grey or bluish grey sky with low ceiling, no clouds, and high humidity.	Very slow speed, losses may occur.

(2) DARKNESS. Pigeons never lose their initial fear of flying at night, but it is possible to train them to overcome this fear to a great extent. Their natural instinct and intelligence will come to their aid. Night operation, however, is considered impracticable for the Army pigeons because of the highly mobile tactics of modern warfare.

(3) INJURY. Injuries are commonly caused by improper handling, predatory birds (such as hawks), enemy shellfire, or obstacles pigeons strike in flight. Protect pigeons by destroying all hawks in the vicinity of the lofts with shotguns provided for that purpose. Select safe locations for releasing pigeons. Minor injuries rarely prevent a homing pigeon from returning to its loft as long as they do not hamper it from determining the proper course of flight. When vitally injured, the pigeon will continue its return flight until physically exhausted. Any injury which permanently impairs the eyes or wings of a pigeon makes it unsuitable for any employment except breeding.

SECTION II

DESCRIPTION

6. General Appearance

Pigeons must look healthy, well-balanced, alert, intelligent, and showing abundance of rich feathers and sheen. Figure 1 shows the main parts of the homing pigeon (the right wing is extended for ease of description).

7. Weight

A cock weighs from 14 to 17 ounces; a hen, from 13 to 16 ounces.

8. Plumage

Rich, abundant, and soft plumage should cover the entire body. The color itself is of no importance, but rich shades, with the checkered pattern (if present) standing out brightly and distinctly, usually indicate good health and satisfactory condition. For classification of pigeons according to color see paragraph **26**.

9. Head

The head should be of a medium size, round or oval shaped, of broad structure and strongly set. It should not be tight or drawn at any one place.

A. Bill. The bill should be of medium length with small to medium wattles and set well into the head. No openings should be noticeable when the bill is closed.

B. Eye. See **section VI**.

C. Ear. The ear seems to play an important part in the bird's sense of direction. It includes three parts: external ear, middle ear, and inner ear. At the top of the inner ear there are three semicircular canals which appear to be the nerve conductors of orientation. Although no one knows just what helps homing pigeons find their loft, it is possible that the great sensitiveness of their ears enables them to receive magnetic and atmospheric impression, and thereby to determine direction either at departure or during flight. This theory is based on the fact that atmospheric disturbances often cause the bird temporarily to lose its way.

10. Neck

The neck is of medium length, with no sign of dewlap at the throat. It tapers to a wide, well-sprung chest.

11. Body

A. Breast. The breast (or chest) is broad and full in front; depth of breastbone should not exceed the width.

B. Shoulders. The shoulders are heavy and strongly reinforced with muscles.

C. Back. The back is well-feathered, strong, flat and broad at the shoulders, narrowing toward the rump.

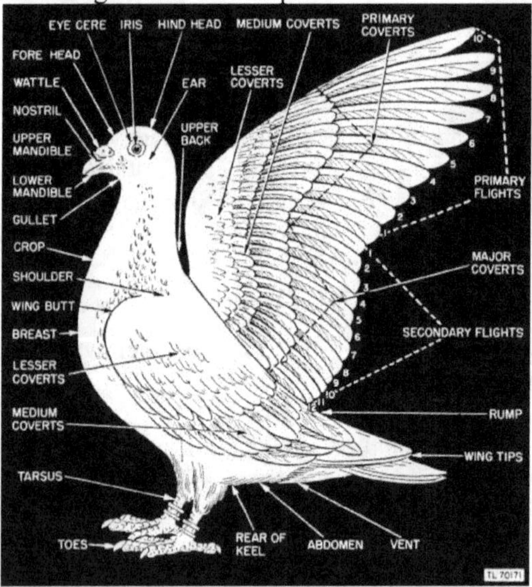

FIGURE 1. PARTS OF HOMING PIGEON.

D. Keel. The keel is strong, arched in front, and of medium length and depth. Width of keel denotes strength.

E. Abdomen. The abdomen is reduced to the smallest proportions.

F. Wings. The wings must be medium-sized, strong, well-proportioned, and rounded at the butt, with plenty of muscle. Primary flights should be of a good width, with plenty of overlapping space and a pronounced curvature towards the body. See I below. Secondary feathers should also be long and wide to provide a good covering for the entire back. Covert feathers should be sturdy and abundant, because they supply additional wing strength, as well as protect pigeons against adverse weather.

G. Pelvic bones. The pelvic bones (or vent bones) are very firm, close together over the vent, and extend toward the keel on each side of the vent. These bones form a body girdle by which the legs are joined to the body.

H. Rump. The rump is wide and continues the line of the back. It is well covered on all sides with fine, soft feathers.

I. Tail feathers. The tail feathers, 12 in number, are short, wide, overlapping, and do not extend farther than ¾ inch beyond the wing tips.

J. Legs. The legs are of medium length and well muscled. Thighs are chubby. Lower leg is red and stout, and toes are short with firm nails.

12. Respiratory Channels (fig. 2)

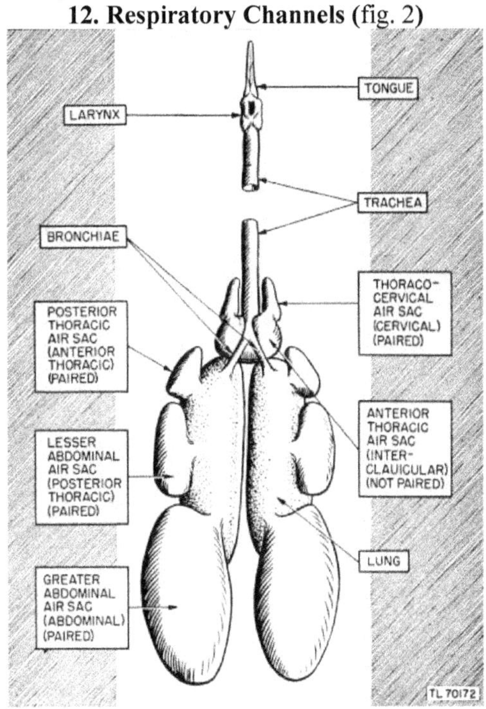

FIGURE 2. RESPIRATORY CHANNELS OF HOMING PIGEON. (AIR SACS ARE NAMED IN ACCORDANCE WITH MCLEOD AND WAGERS. OTHER NAMES ARE GIVEN IN PARENTHESIS.)

Respiratory channels are highly developed, enabling the pigeon to fly continuously from 12 to 15 hours. Air circulates through the bronchial tubes and lungs and also through nine air sacs, from which other small, irregular cavities extend under the skin between the muscles, and even

into the inside of the bones. These small air sacs contain a reserve of warm air which feeds the lungs during flight when the muscular apparatus consumes a large amount of oxygen. They inflate and collapse alternately, acting as a lift and force pump which renews air in the lungs.

13. Digestive Organs

Digestive organs of the pigeon are shown in figure 3 (for functions see **par. 50B**).

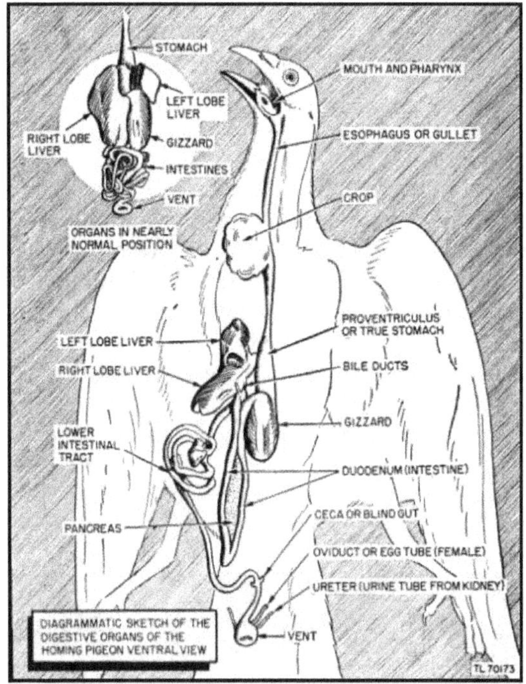

FIGURE 3. DIGESTIVE ORGANS OF HOMING PIGEON.

14. Bloom or Milt

This white, chalky powder is one of the means provided by nature to protect feathers against moisture during flight. When the pigeon bathes, the bloom is deposited in the form of a white scum on the top of the water. If a bird is caught and held closely, the bloom rubs off, leaving a white substance on the clothes. Absence of bloom is a symptom of poor health.

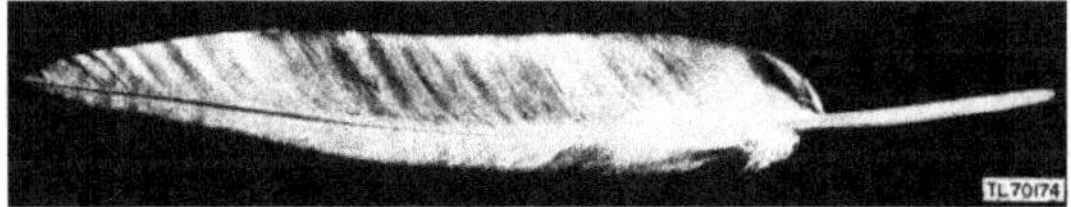

FIGURE 4. A FLIGHT.

15. Molt

Molting is nature's way of shedding feathers and furnishing new ones for the entire body. Thus, feathers lost or injured the preceding year are replenished, and a perfect coat is insured for the coming year. An imperfect molt indicates an unhealthy condition which will reduce the pigeon's efficiency and result in the breeding of inferior offspring.

A. Time of molt. Every pigeon should molt once a year. Mated pigeons start molting approximately 1 week after the second set of eggs has been laid in the new season. Unmated old pigeons ordinarily begin molting in May or June. The time young birds molt depends primarily on the date of hatch. Those hatched during the early part of July begin with head and neck feathers very soon after leaving the nest, and later during the year partially molt all feathers. The process is completed the following summer. Various influences hasten or retard molting. For example, exceptionally warm weather may hasten it. Poor health retards and may prevent a complete molt. Early breeding ordinarily hastens the process, while late breeding tends to delay it.

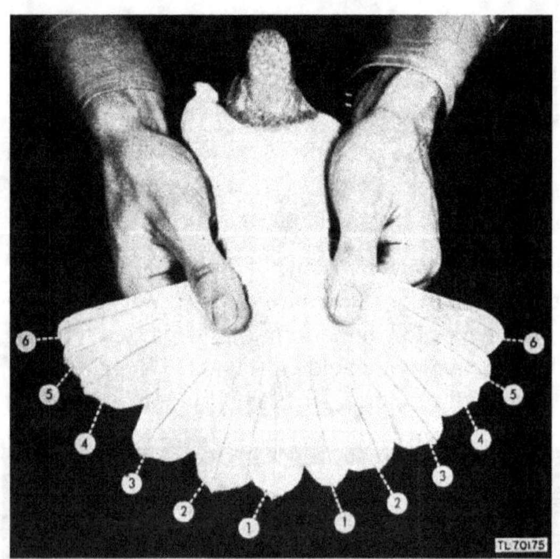

FIGURE 5. TAIL FEATHERS OF HOMING PIGEON.

B. Order of molt. Feathers are shed in the following order (see **par. 16** and **fig. 1**):

(1) Primary flight No. 1 is shed first, and new feathers begin to grow in its place.

(2) As soon as new feathers are one-half to three-quarters grown, remaining primary flights are shed in numerical order.

(3) When flights Nos. 5 or 6 have been shed, molt spreads to neck and shoulders.

(4) By the time flights Nos. 6 or 7 have been shed, the tail-molt begins with feathers No. 2 (**fig. 8**), then continues in the following numerical order: 1, 3, 4, 6, and 5.

(5) When the last flights have been shed, the molt is practically complete, except for a few fine body feathers.

C. CARE DURING MOLT. The molt is a great physical drain on pigeons; therefore, if practicable, hard flying and breeding activities should be temporarily abandoned during this period. Exercise flights should be only as long as is necessary for the pigeon's health. When weather permits, the birds should be allowed to bathe regularly, because this will soften the skin and help feathers drop. The only sure method of correcting an unsatisfactory molt is to restore the pigeon to a healthy, vigorous physical condition. No attempt should be made to aid the molt by plucking the next feathers in order, as in all probability the new feathers will be inferior, or may not even appear. The substance which creates new feathers is lacking in the sockets for about 2 months after the molt is completed. During the molting period, it is especially necessary that birds be fed rich, oily, easily digested food such as grain (hemp, canary, flax or linseed) and greens. This food will keep weight up to normal and insure a good growth of feathers.

16. Varieties of Feathers

Feathers grow in definite areas on the body. These feathered areas or strips are known as pterylae. Bare spaces in between are called apterylae. Feathers are divided into four types: contour feathers, hair feathers, fluff feathers, and down feathers.

A. Contour feathers. Contour feathers are large feathers covering the pigeon's body. When the bird is not in flight or excited, they lie close to its body, normally overlapping and presenting a smooth outer surface. The larger ones are the flight and tail feathers. The average pigeon has 12 main tail feathers; on each wing there are 10 primary flights and 12 secondary flights. The bases of these large feathers are covered by shorter feathers called coverts. These give a rounded, smooth, and continuous line to the body.

The main tail feathers act as a rudder in flight, controlling the bird's direction. Flying is possible because every flight feather overlaps, presenting a solid surface on the downbeat of the wing. Besides, flight feathers provide lift and pull for the bird's propulsion. On the upbeat of the wing, the large flight feathers rotate in such a manner as to cut through the air with little resistance, and at the same time to permit escape of air.

The general structure of a contour feather can be best observed in a primary flight from the wing or a large rectrix from the tail. The stiff, hollow, cylindrical portion emerging from the skin is called the quill. The bare quill proper extends only to the webbed portion of the feather. It has a small hole (inferior umbilicus) at the end, penetrating the skin.

Nourishment for the feather passes through this opening. The expanded portion of the feather, from the tip to the quill, is known as the vane. The central portion of the vane, which is called the shaft, is solid. Extending laterally from the shaft is a web or webbing composed of barbs or rays. These rays are blade-like in structure. The web of most feathers is generally wider on one side of the shaft than on the other. The barbs are connected by a series of cross structures called barbules which can be seen only with the aid of magnifying lens. To see the barbs, however, apply a slight tension on the webbing of the feather, causing it to spread apart. The invisible barbules will split if too much tension is applied. Barbs can be repaired so that little or no evidence of the split can be detected, by stroking the feather between the index finger and thumb. Pigeons repair a split in the barb by squeezing oil from the oil duct with their beak, and then spreading it on the injured feather.

Feather textures vary greatly with the breed of the bird and the part of the body from which they grow. When selecting homing pigeons, try to select those with strong, firm feathers.

B. Hair feathers. Also known as filoplumes, hair feathers are hair-like structures interspersed among the regular body feathers. They are so fine that they are usually overlooked.

C. Fluff feathers. Sometimes called semiplumes, fluff feathers are soft and fluffy because of the absence of a rigid feather shaft and barbules in their web. The barbs are also long, soft, and fluffy, and present a downy appearance. Fluff feathers grow only on certain parts of the body.

D. Down feathers. Down feathers are the soft, hairy, yellow feathers on young pigeons. They are extremely fine, almost filamentous in structure. These feathers drop off all through the period of the young bird's growth; a few, however, may remain after complete feathering has taken place.

SECTION III

CARE

17. Loft

Pigeons are housed in lofts which may be buildings or vehicles designed and equipped for that purpose. The loft includes all the equipment, accessories and utilities necessary for the care of pigeons (figs. 6, 7, and 8). Perches are placed on the sides of loft walls. When a pigeon is "settled" to a loft, that loft becomes its home.

A. An AVIARY is the part of the loft where pigeons can be given sunlight. It is usually built with wire netting on the sides and roof.

B. The TRAP is a specially constructed opening which permits the pigeon to enter but not to leave the loft. When a pigeon enters the loft this way, it is said to have "trapped." A trap which permits the pigeon to enter and leave at will is called an "open trap." A landing board is placed in front of the trap upon which pigeons alight when about to enter the loft.

C. A SETTLING CAGE of wire which is built to fit over the roof and landing board of the loft, is used to aid in settling and training pigeons to trap.

18. Preparation of Loft to Receive Pigeons

The first step in preparing to receive a shipment of pigeons is to arrange for their housing. If it is the initial stock for a loft, the entire loft will be available. In the case of subsequent shipment, place new stock in a separate compartment for a period of observation. In order to anticipate arrival of birds, maintain contact with the agency making delivery. Then proceed as follows:

A. Clean the loft.

B. In good weather keep front of the loft open so that plenty of sunlight and air can enter.

C. To keep drafts out during extreme cold and windy weather, cover openings of the loft with porous materials which will allow passage of air and will not interfere with the camouflage appearance.

D. Spread a small quantity of coarse sand on the floor of the loft to aid cleanliness and to supplement the grit.

E. Provide 10 percent more perching space than is necessary for the number of incoming birds.

19. Receipt of Pigeons at Loft

To receive pigeons at a loft, proceed as follows:

A. Immediately upon their arrival transfer the birds to the loft from the crates or baskets in which they were transported. The pigeons may have completed a lengthy trip and be in comparatively poor condition because of delays in travel or lack of proper care and attention.

B. Immediately after the birds have been transferred to the loft, carefully examine and handle each pigeon, separating the healthy from the sickly. Place the healthy birds in a compartment where they can obtain

plenty of fresh drinking water, and feed them sparingly. Isolate the birds which appear sick until they are fully recovered.

FIGURE 6. STATIONARY LOFT.

FIGURE 7. LOFT PG-46-A.

C. It is imperative that the pigeons be vaccinated against pigeon pox if they were not vaccinated prior to shipment.

D. Thereafter water, feed, and provide bathing water according to instructions in paragraphs 20 to 23, inclusive.

E. Make an exact inventory of the pigeons, noting band markings, colors, special markings, and physical condition of each bird.

F. Become familiar with the pigeons while they are confined. Accustom them to the presence of caretakers and to feeding at definite times.

G. Begin training of the new birds immediately. The longer the time between their arrival at their new home and the beginning of their training, the more difficult it will be for them to be trained properly.

20. Watering

A. The health of a pigeon depends more upon pure drinking water than upon any other factor; therefore, keep plenty of fresh water available at all times.

B. The homing pigeon does not drink like most other birds. The pigeon places its bill into the water, and takes a long, deep draft like a horse. For this reason, keep the depth of the water in the drinking fountain not less than 1½ inches deep. Always supply water in a fountain or other receptacle which will prevent bathing. Fountains PG-37-C provide excellent watering facilities for the birds and are constructed to reduce contamination to a minimum (**fig. 9**).

FIGURE 8. LOFT PG-68/TB.

C. In warm weather, change the water three times a day, cleaning the container thoroughly each time. In cool weather, twice a day may be sufficient, provided the water can be kept clean. Water containing impurities gives the pigeon a sour crop or acute indigestion. If a sanitary water supply is not readily available, use drinking water purified for troops. When it is necessary to use water of doubtful purity, add a sufficient amount of potassium permanganate until a light pink color is attained. Empty drinking fountains at night in cold weather so that the water will not freeze. Having running water in the drinking fountain is not advisable as it is usually cool and may cause diarrhea during hot weather.

FIGURE 9. FOUNTAIN PG-37-C IN LOFT.

21. Feeding

A. General. The health and general physical condition of a pigeon largely depend on the amount of food, time of feeding, and the kind of food provided. Pigeons should not refuse food unless they have just been fed. They will be alert, active, happy, and much more manageable if kept a little hungry. It is easy to overfeed pigeons so that they become sluggish and listless. Many good pigeons have been spoiled by overfeeding. The pigeoneer should hand-feed the birds and watch them closely while they are eating because their appetite reflects their general health and condition. Sick birds may be discovered by their failure to eat. Pigeons become

better acquainted with the pigeoneer through hand-feeding, and he in turn can keep them alert and under control.

B. Method. Feed pigeons TWICE a day during training, light feeding in the morning and heavier in the evening. After each exercise, training, or other flight, call the pigeons into the loft and give them a small quantity of feed as a reward. While the pigeons are taking their morning exercise, clean the loft and place in it a fresh supply of grit and drinking water. Call the birds in when they have completed their exercises, then scatter the food slowly on the sand-covered floor as the birds enter through the trap. Scatter the feed, a handful at a time. Wait until the pigeons have eaten nearly all the feed before distributing another handful. The feed should be well scattered so that individual birds do not get all of the choice grains. No harm is done if the pigeons eat some of the sand, providing it is clean, as sand supplements grit as an aid to digestion. There are several reasons why pigeons should be fed only a handful at a time. If the whole amount of grain for one feeding is thrown on the floor at once, the actual amount needed cannot be estimated exactly. If the amount estimated was too little, the pigeons are underfed; if the amount was excessive, the grain not immediately consumed becomes contaminated and may cause sickness if eaten later. Another reason for scattering feed in small quantities is to prevent the pigeons from picking out the kinds of grain they particularly like and leaving those which contain food elements they need for proper development. Pigeons always drink immediately after feeding. When the first pigeon stops eating and takes a drink, it is a sign that the pigeons have had enough food so do not scatter any more grain.

C. Breeding pigeons. Parent pigeons feed their young in the nest by ejecting food from their own crops into the youngster's crop. Therefore, when young pigeons are in the nest, return in about 30 minutes after the initial feeding and offer additional food to the parents. When the youngsters are approximately 18 days of age, start placing a handful of grain each day in the back corner of the nest compartment out of the way of the droppings. The parent pigeons will eat a few grains in the presence of the youngsters. The youngsters will imitate their parents and thus learn to eat by themselves more rapidly.

22. Pigeon Feed

The diet for a pigeon should include legumes (peas and vetch), seeds, cereal grains, green foods, and grit. The seeds and grains are fed as an ordinary diet in the form of a feed mixture, but grit is fed separately. Feed must be of a specific grade and mixture to assure the pigeon of proper growth, a generally healthy condition, and enough energy to endure the hardships of messenger flights. Pigeon feed, which is a perishable item, must be grown under prescribed conditions from the finest quality seed, harvested, cleaned, stored, and then mixed when required. When harvested, grain or seed is likely to contain many impurities like chaff, weed seeds, weevils, or other injurious insects, kernels which are dead or damaged, and excessive moisture. Practically all of these impurities must be removed before the feed is suitable for use. Mixing must be accomplished under conditions that will insure uniformity. The word "feed" as used below will refer to either mixed feed, grain, or seeds, as applicable. A single grain or seed will be referred to as a "kernel."

A. Suitable feed. Feed should—

(1) Be sound and have a natural odor, without traces of sour, musty, or foreign odors.

(2) Be well matured and of good natural color, without a noticeable amount of dead or damaged kernels.

(3) Be free of dirt, dust, or foreign material, beyond a slight trace.

(4) Be free from live weevils or other insects and the defects caused by them.

(5) Be free-flowing, without traces of webbyness.

(6) Not contain excessive moisture as determined by the field test described in B (5) below.

B. Defective pigeon feed. Defects in feed can be recognized by smell, visual inspection, or laboratory test. Feed is unsuitable for use if it has any of the following defects:

(1) UNSOUND. This condition may be detected by a sour or musty odor or by an "off color" appearance.

(2) FOREIGN MATERIALS. Chaff, dirt, dust, stones, etc., can be detected by visual inspection.

(3) WEBBYNESS. When feed has been, or is infected, with injurious insects it is likely to be webby. The feed will cling together in small balls by webs similar to cobwebs. It may also have an objectionable odor.

(4) DEAD OR DAMAGED KERNELS. Kernels that have sprouted, been bored by insects, or are discolored as a result of frost, fermentation, or immaturity, can be detected by a visual inspection.

(5) MOISTURE. Small amounts of moisture cannot be detected without a laboratory test. However, a field method which may be employed to determine roughly the moisture content of feed is to place a few of the kernels on a flat surface and then strike them a few times with a hammer or similar tool. If the feed tested does not contain an excessive amount of moisture, the kernels will crumble into small pieces like "corn meal." If an excessive amount of moisture is present the kernels will become pulpy. When performing this test, remember that hulled oats, flax seed, hemp seed, and vetch, because of their oil content, will become pulpy even though their moisture content is within required limits.

C. Harmful insects. The two most harmful insects to pigeon feed are weevils and grain moths.

(1) WEEVILS. Weevils are small beetle-type insects which vary in color from brown to black. They eat by boring holes into the portion of the kernel containing the nutritive elements. Weevils can be detected by the test described in **I(2)(B)** below.

(2) GRAIN MOTHS. These small moths vary in color from buff to grayish or yellowish brown. During the larva stage they gnaw their way into the kernel and then eat the inside portion to secure nourishment for growth. When fully grown they eat their way out of the kernel. The presence of moths in feed can be detected by the holes they leave in kernels.

D. Feed mixtures. Various seeds and grains are mixed in specified percentages to acquire a feed mixture of certain required amounts of proteins, carbohydrates, and fats. Factors determining the type of feed mixture used are climatic conditions, the way in which the pigeon is used, and the condition of the bird. Different mixtures are fed during the breeding and molting period, while training or conditioning, or while the pigeons are used for messenger service. Use of feed mixtures is as follows:

(1) BREEDING FEED is used to maintain a healthy physical condition in parent pigeons, and at the same time supply essential food elements necessary to raise strong young pigeons.

(2) TRAINING AND CONDITIONING FEED builds and maintains a physical condition suitable for short distance messenger service during the training period.

(3) SPECIAL FEED supplies energy and replaces the body tissues consumed by the pigeon when it is continuously used for messenger service.

(4) MOLTING FEED, a supplementary feed mixture containing hemp, canary, flax, and rape, insures good feathers and keeps the weight of the pigeon normal by supplying rich, oily, and easily digested feed.

E. Analysis. The three principal properties of feed that are necessary for development and maintenance of a sound physical condition are proteins, carbohydrates, and fats.

(1) PROTEINS contribute a large portion of the elements necessary for maintaining the pigeon's health, muscular and respiratory system, and the organs essential to flying. The most important feeds in the protein class are peas and vetch.

(2) CARBOHYDRATES supply energy. The portion of carbohydrates not used immediately changes to "fat" and is held in reserve by the pigeon to be drawn upon when it is being used continuously for messenger service. The most important suppliers of carbohydrates are rice, kaffir, wheat, corn, and hulled oats.

(3) FATS keep the pigeon warm and also build a reserve supply of energy. The feeds which furnish fats are rape, flax, and hemp seed.

F. Analysis chart. The following chart gives a comparative analysis of the grains and seeds used for pigeon feed:

ANALYSIS CHART

Stock No.	Ingredient	Moisture	Ash	Crude protein	Carbohydrates		Fat
					Crude fiber	Nitrogen free extract	
9A705	Buckwheat, unofficial **2**	12.6	2.0	10.0	8.7	64.5	2.2
9A747	Seed, canary, 99% pure, unofficial **2**	7.0	5.5	17.2	5.7	59.1	5.5
9A747.1	Seed, flax, 99% pure, U. S. No. 1 **1**	9.2	4.3	22.6	7.0	23.2	33.7
9A876.1	Corn, American, small grain, U. S. No. 1 **1**	12.9	1.3	9.3	1.9	70.3	4.3
9A1360	Seed, hemp, sterilized, 99% pure, unofficial **2**	8.0	2.0	10.0	14.0	45.0	21.0
9A1550	Kaffir, U. S. No. 1 **1**	9.4	1.6	11.1	2.1	72.6	3.2
9A1765	Seed, millet, 99% pure, unofficial **2**	9.1	3.3	11.8	7.8	64.7	3.3
9A1787	Oats, hulled, table grade, unofficial **2**	8.4	1.8	16.0	1.5	65.5	6.8
9A1848	Peas, Canada, U. S. No. 1 **1**	9.2	3.4	23.0	5.5	57.8	1.1
9A1848.1	Peas, maple, unofficial **2**	11.0	2.5	21.9	5.5	58.2	0.9
9A1848.2	Peas, white, First and Best, U. S. No. 1 **1**	9.1	3.3	11.8	7.8	64.7	3.3

9A1901	Seed, rape, large, sweet, 99% pure, unofficial **2**	14.0	3.9	19.4	7.8	16.4	38.5
9A1940	Rice, whole, extra fancy, U. S. No. 1 **1**	12.4	0.4	7.4	0.2	79.2	0.4
9A2600	Vetch, common, unofficial **2**	13.7	3.3	25.4	5.4	50.7	1.5
9A2800	Wheat, hard red or durum, U. S. No. 1 **1**	10.6	1.8	12.3	2.4	71.1	1.8

<u>1</u> "U. S. No. 1 Grade" complies with standards for that grade established by the U. S. Department of Agriculture.

<u>2</u> "Unofficial grade" indicates grain or seed "well-matured, sound, clean, and of good natural color and odor" as certified to by a recognized Official Grain Inspection Agency.

NOTE. The above analysis of ingredients for pigeon feed are averages. Climatic conditions or the locality in which the grain or seed is grown may slightly alter this analysis.

G. Green food. Certain amounts of this food are essential for the pigeon's digestive organs to function properly. Crisp young lettuce, kale (preferably curly), and chickweed are the best green foods for pigeons. Pigeons prefer green stuff sprinkled with a little table salt. While green food is in season, give the pigeons as much of it as they will eat about three times a week. The preferred method for feeding this type of food is to suspend it in bunches on the inside of the loft about 4 inches from the floor.

H. Formulas. (1) The formulas for the various feed mixtures are listed below under their suggested use. It must be remembered that the factor governing the use of these feed mixtures will be climate and existing conditions.

BREEDING

Stock No. 9A1219.2

25%	American corn
10%	Kaffir
25%	Canada peas or white peas, First and Best

5%	Millet seed
20%	Vetch
15%	Wheat, hard red or durum

MOLTING

Stock No. 9A1219.8

15%	Rice, whole
20%	Canary seed
15%	Flax seed
20%	Hemp seed
20%	Millet seed
10%	Rape seed

TRAINING OR CONDITIONING

Stock No. 9A1219.5

3.5%	Buckwheat
25.0%	American corn
5.0%	Kaffir
2.5%	Oats, hulled
12.5%	Canada peas or white peas, First and Best
12.5%	Peas, maple
5.0%	Rice, whole
2.5%	Canary seed
5.0%	Hemp seed
5.0%	Millet seed
15.0%	Vetch
6.5%	Wheat, hard red or durum

Note. This mixture may also be used for a breeding feed.

Stock No. 9A1219.6

35%	American corn

5%	Oats, hulled
10%	Canada peas or white peas, First and Best
15%	Maple peas
5%	Rice, whole
5%	Hemp seed
15%	Vetch
10%	Wheat, hard red or durum

Note. This mixture may also be used for a breeding feed.

SPECIAL

Stock No. 9A1219.4

25%	American corn
25%	Canada peas or white peas, First and Best
30%	Maple peas
20%	Vetch

Stock No. 9A1219.7

10%	American corn
5%	Hulled oats
20%	Canada peas or white peas, First and Best
25%	Maple peas
5%	Rice, whole
5%	Hemp seed
20%	Vetch
10%	Wheat, hard red or durum

Note. Recommended for tropical climate.

(2) The following chart gives a comparative analysis of the above mixtures:

Stock No.	Moisture	Ash	Crude protein	Crude fiber	Carbohydrates	Fat
					Nitrogen free extract	
9A1219.2	11.26	2.42	16.71	3.89	63.33	2.39
9A1219.4	11.57	2.58	19.73	4.58	59.63	1.91
9A1219.5	11.27	2.27	15.76	4.50	62.76	3.44
9A1219.6	11.64	2.06	15.56	3.87	63.32	3.55
9A1219.7	11.12	2.49	18.98	4.78	59.87	2.76
9A1219.8	9.46	3.25	14.24	7.36	50.76	14.93

I. Storage and fumigation. Pigeon feed procured in accordance with U. S. Army Specification 24-17-C, is of the finest ingredients obtainable in accordance with U. S. Department of Agriculture standards, and is processed prior to packing. If stored properly this feed will not become contaminated. Improper storage, however, counteracts the precautions taken to procure best quality feed. Therefore, the instructions below have been prepared to safeguard the original quality of the feed during storage.

(1) PROPER METHOD OF STORAGE. The larval, pupal and adult stages of injurious grain insects are inactive in a temperature of 50° F. or lower. Thus the first and the most important rule is to store feed in a COOL, DRY PLACE, on a platform at least 6 inches above the floor.

(A) There are several simple methods of stacking bagged feed. One way is to stand the first tier of bags on end on a movable floor of narrow boards nailed to joists. Bags should be set far enough apart to admit air and light. The air keeps the bags dry and the light discourages rats. Other tiers of bags are laid flat, each tier at right angles to the previous tier, to admit air and light (**fig. 10**). A second method is to lay a tier of bags flat on two parallel timbers, each tier laid at right angles to the previous tier (**fig. 10**).

(B) After feed has been stacked, it must be protected against rats. An inexpensive protective method is to construct a wooden framework inside the building where the feed is to be stored, and to cover it completely with ¼-inch wire mesh. The size of the wire mesh inclosure depends on the amount of feed to be stored.

FIGURE 10. METHODS OF STACKING BAGS.
(2) EXAMINATION FOR CONTAMINATION.

Feed stored in a hot climate or in buildings where injurious grain insects are present is likely to become infested.

Therefore feed should be visually examined bimonthly for presence of moths or adult insects.

(A) Take the temperature of the feed by inserting a thermometer into the feed, especially in the bags at the center of the pile. If it exceeds 75° F. make a closer and more frequent examination.

(B) A simple and practical test to discover the presence of insects is to place a quantity of the questionable feed in a sieve with 1/16-inch wire mesh (sieve PG-35), and shake over a white cloth or paper. Examine screenings and if insects are present, fumigate the feed according to instructions in (3) below to prevent further damage and ultimate ruin.

(3) FUMIGATION. There are three methods for fumigating contaminated pigeon feed available to pigeon units.

FIGURE 11. BATH PAN PG-38.

(A) Quartermaster, fumigation and bath companies (T/O & E 10-257) have facilities, such as portable methyl bromide fumigation chambers, for delousing clothing which may be used for fumigating pigeon feed. These units are generally assigned to posts, camps, or stations and to theaters of operations, and their services may be obtained. To use their equipment,

load chamber with bags of contaminated feed, seal, and charge it with a 2-pound can of methyl bromide, Stock Number 51M892 (see Quartermaster supplement of the Federal Standard Stock Catalog). Feed should remain in the chamber for at least 24 hours. Temperature of the interior of the chamber should be maintained at a minimum of 70° F.

(B) If a portable fumigation chamber is not available, a building which can be tightly sealed, like those used for training purposes in the Chemical Warfare Service, may be used. The feed should be loaded into the vault so that the entire floor space is utilized. Seal vault tightly and apply methyl bromide from the outside of the vault through a ¼-inch diameter copper tubing at the top of the chamber. The connection between the tubing and the methyl bromide container should allow no leakage. The feed should remain in the vault for at least 24 hours. The temperature of the interior of the vault should be maintained at a minimum of 75° F. for best results. Use at least 1 pound of methyl bromide per 1,000 cubic feet of space. After the 24-hour exposure period, open vault and air it for a few hours before removing feed. Methyl bromide is toxic to human beings. Therefore, before opening or entering the vault after the exposure period, the fumigator should wear a gas mask type M9A1, with a standard service canister.

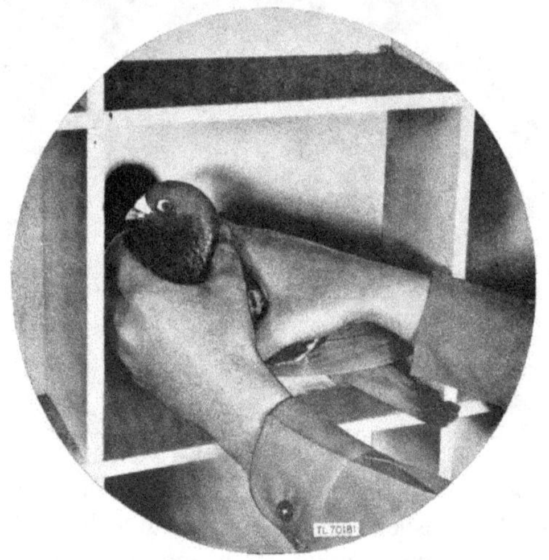

FIGURE 12. CATCHING PIGEON IN LOFT.

(C) If a portable fumigation chamber or gas tight vault is not available, "tarpaulin method" of fumigation may be used. Sweep clear the floor

(preferably cement) where the feed is to be placed for fumigation. Stack the bags of feed in a square area to a height of 5 or 6 feet. After the feed is stacked, center four bags of feed in an upright position on top of the pile to form a gas expansion dome. Throw a tarpaulin which is large enough to cover completely the entire pile of feed over the pile. Allow a minimum margin of 2 feet on the floor for sealing. The tarpaulin should be of treated material, preferably rubberized, to prevent leakage and to be impervious to the fumigant. Seal the marginal excess of tarpaulin with filled bags or weights. The fumigant is released from the container through a tubing extending from the container under the tarpaulin to the top of the gas expansion dome. The same type of fumigant, dosage, exposure, and temperature required for vault or chamber fumigation are employed, and the same precautions are observed when removing the tarpaulin after the exposure period. If circumstances prevent a tight sealing of the tarpaulin use an increased amount of fumigant to compensate for leakage.

J. Use and preparation of grit. Grit is a prepared mixture which serves as a mechanical grinder for the food in the pigeon's gizzard and assists in assimilation. Grit also purifies the crop and supplies lime for bone building and forming of egg shells. Many grit mixtures are available, most of which contain crushed oyster shell, gravel, sand, small sea shells, crushed limestone, salt, charcoal, and other ingredients.

(1) Between 5 and 10 percent of the food fed a pigeon should be grit. Normally 5 percent is sufficient, except during the breeding season when as much as 10 percent may be fed since the parent pigeons pump grit into the youngsters when they start eating grains.

(2) A preferred grit is made as follows:

(A) Thoroughly mix (in the manner of mixing mortar) 20 pounds of medium granite grit, 20 pounds of medium oyster shell, 20 pounds of medium crushed limestone, 5 pounds of medium charcoal, and 1/8 pound of oxide of iron (hematite). Then dissolve 3 pounds of table salt in boiling water and add just enough of this solution to the mixture to dampen it thoroughly. Do not add too much water. Thoroughly mix the whole preparation and allow to dry before feeding to birds.

(B) Each of the various ingredients in the mixture has a purpose. The granite is a grinder and pulverizes the food; the oxide of iron has a beneficial effect upon the blood and acts as a tonic; the charcoal purifies the crop, acting as a stomachic, that is, strengthening or stimulating action of the stomach. Limestone provides the materials for strengthening the bones. The oyster shells contribute lime which enters into the composition of bones and egg shells.

(3) The grit mixtures used are listed in the Signal Corps General Catalog, as Stock Nos. 9A1321 (color red), and 9A1322 (color natural) "Seashell" or equal.

(4) Keep grit in the loft constantly except during the 24 hours before the pigeons are to be sent away to a point 50 or more miles distant for immediate liberation. Since grit contains salt and minerals which cause thirst, pigeons might land en route for water, thereby losing valuable time and exposing themselves to the danger of being shot or captured. Place the grit in a wooden box designed so that the pigeons cannot easily

introduce foreign matter into the mixture. Inspect the box daily and remove all foreign matter. Refill the grit container with dry grit as needed. Once a week empty the grit container and clean it thoroughly. Add a

fresh supply and destroy the old grit. Always keep an ample supply of grit in stock at the loft.

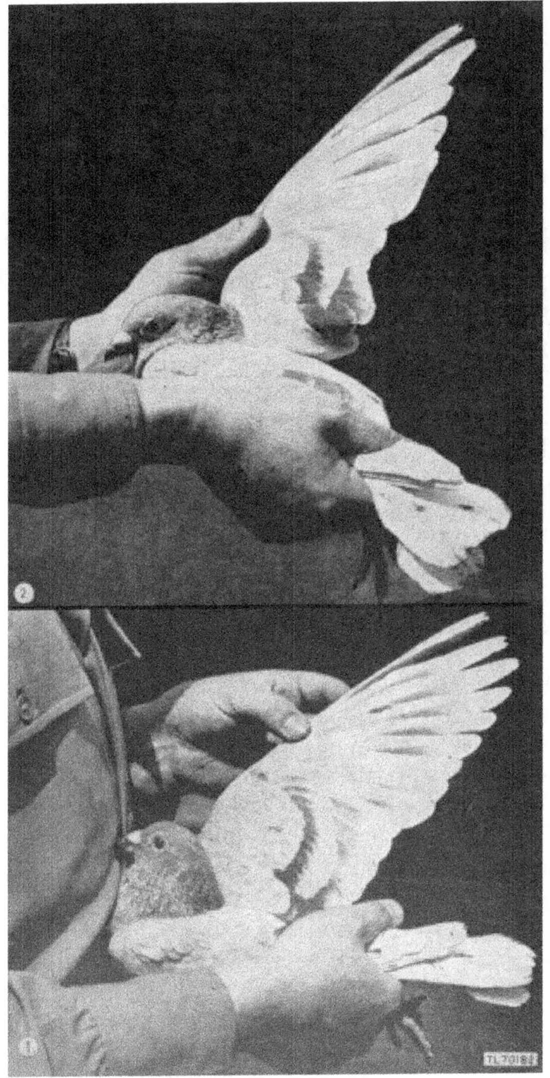

(1) CORRECT(2) INCORRECT
FIGURE 13. HOLDING PIGEON FOR INSPECTION.

FIGURE 14. CATCHING PIGEON IN CRATE.

K. Allowance of feed and grit. (1) The annual allowance of feed mixture is 52 pounds for each pigeon because the average pigeon, including those breeding and those not breeding, consumes 1 pound of grain per week.

(2) The annual allowance of grit is 6 pounds a pigeon.

23. Bathing

A. No other class of fowl, except the duck family, enjoys a bath as much as pigeons. Pigeons that are kept clean have less trouble with mites or feather lice. The use of a quassia chip solution in the bath water is excellent for keeping pigeons free from lice and should be used once a week. To prepare the solution, boil one pound of quassia chips in 2 gallons of water for 20 minutes. Strain off the liquid and use 2 quarts of this solution to 3 gallons of bath water.

B. As far as practicable, provide bath water daily during warm weather but omit in freezing weather. Approximately 1 hour after the morning feeding prepare the bath pan PG-38 and leave it in position about 1 hour. Scrub the pan thoroughly after the pigeons have finished bathing. During the breeding season provide the bath after the morning feeding as usual, but on alternate days provide the bath in the early afternoon. This method enables both cocks and hens to bathe every other day (see **par. 44<u>A</u>**).

24. Catching and Handling

Great care must be exercised when catching and handling pigeons because their flying ability depends upon their physical condition, and awkward and improper handling may result in the loss or breaking of tail and flight feathers. The correct methods of catching and handling birds are shown in figures 12 and 13.

A. Catching in crate. To catch a pigeon in a crate or container, gently force it to the corner or end of the container and place palm of the hand in a firm position over pigeon's shoulders (**fig. 14**); then turn the bird around

(facing bird to door or entrance) and gently grasp it between both hands for lifting from crate. Bring pigeon to normal position in front of the waistline. Pigeons must be taken head first from all crates to prevent injury to the feathers.

(1) CORRECT(2) INCORRECT
FIGURE 15. CRATING A PIGEON.

B. Catching in loft. This should be done with great care and ease as both the physical and feather condition of a pigeon may be impaired by awkward handling. There are several good methods for catching pigeons. The following one has been found to be satisfactory when carried out properly:

(1) Always catch pigeons while in nests or on perches (**fig. 15**). Approach pigeon calmly, avoiding sudden movements that might frighten it.

(2) Grasp bird by a quick movement of the hands. Catch it from the front, with the thumbs on its back and fingers under its body.

Caution: Never attempt to catch birds in the aviary, or when they are flying about the loft.

C. Inspecting birds. When examining the wings, back, or tail feathers of a pigeon, always hold its chest or front portion against your body (**fig. 12**) for security. To examine the head, eyes, or bill, place the bird properly in one hand using the other hand as a front or side support, leaving fingers free for examination.

D. Crating birds. Hold the bird with your thumb across its back and its legs between your first two fingers; place the palm of the other hand over the front part of the pigeon, extend fingers downward in the direction of the keel (**fig. 15**), and guide the bird into the crate. Do not release until bird's feet are firmly on crate floor. Avoid crating birds with one hand only.

SECTION IV

LOFT MANAGEMENT AND RECORDS

25. Routine

A pigeoneer in charge of a loft can best care for his pigeons by observing the following daily routine in loft management:

A. Upon entering the loft, make a general inspection to see that everything is in order.

B. Sweep or scrape all sand and droppings and sift through a fine screen. Add new sand and spread in a thin layer.

C. Provide fresh drinking water (**Par. 20**).

D. Provide bath water (**par. 23**).

E. Conduct prescribed exercise and other training for pigeons according to schedule. This may include all types of flights.

F. Post loft records.

G. Prepare daily quantity of feed and give prescribed portions.

H. Inspect all pigeons as to condition, health, mating, breeding, etc., whenever required.

I. Carry out any special instructions given for the day.

26. Classification of Pigeon Colors

A. The color of the upper body and wings determines the principal color classification of pigeons. In addition to principal color classification (see <u>B</u>**(1)** below), include the following classifications when applicable:

(1) If any of the primary flights are white, the pigeon is classed as a "white flight." Unless the flights are pure white the classification "white flight" is not made.

(2) If all the coverts exhibit a light gray fringe on their outer edges, presenting a checkered appearance rather than a solid color, the pigeon is classed as "checkered."

(3) When a pigeon has white patches of feathers on its head, it is classed as "pied." If these white patches extend to its body, it is classed as "splash."

(4) If a pigeon exhibits one or two white feathers about the eyes, it is classed as "tick."

B. Main color classifications for pigeons and their authorized abbreviations follow:

(1) PRINCIPAL COLORS.

TYPE	ABBREVIATION	DESCRIPTION
Black	(Blk)	All feathers are black.
Blue	(B)	All feathers are grayish blue, generally with two black bars on each wing.
Silver	(Sil)	All feathers are deep grayish silver, generally with two red bars on each wing.
Red	(R)	All feathers are a solid brownish red (often called chocolate).

(2) CHECKERS.

TYPE	ABBREVIATION	DESCRIPTION
Black Checker	(Blk ch)	Principal color black with dark gray or checker markings on rump and underpart of body.
Dark checker	(Dk ch)	Similar to black checker but showing more distinct checker markings on the wing.
Blue checker	(B ch)	Principally blue with checker markings on the body and wings.
Red checker	(R ch)	Principally red with checker markings on the body and wings.
Dun	(Dun)	Similar to silver except principal color is of a darker shade.

Mealy	(Mly)	Similar to dun except that they do not have sharply defined red markings on the wings.
Grizzle	(Griz)	Principal colors consist of red, black, and white mottled together. (Often the black or red colors are not present.) Birds also will be found with grizzle markings around the head and neck only. However, these birds will be classified as grizzles and the wing markings may be indicated as well.

(3) COMBINATIONS. Examples of combinations of colorings and markings, together with their authorized abbreviations, are—

(A) Black with white flights pied (Blk wft pd).

(B) Red with white flights (R wft).

(C) Blue pied (B pd).

(D) Black splash (Blk spl).

(E) Red checkered splash (R Ch spl).

(F) Blue checkered tick (B Ch tk).

(G) Blue with white flights (B wft).

(H) Checkered (Ch).

(I) Grizzle with blue wing markings (B griz).

27. Records and Reports

The records and reports required for each pigeon unit are Breeding Card, Pigeon Breeding Record, Pigeon Flight Record, Pigeon Pedigree, and Monthly Pigeon Loft Report.

A. Breeding Card, WD SC Form 1132 (**fig. 16**). The breeding card is fastened on the outside of the nest compartment as soon as the cock and the hen are mated and take possession of the nest. It remains there during the breeding activities of the particular pair of parent pigeons. The data provide the initial identification record of the youngsters and permit a careful check on the progress of their development. Entries must be timely, accurate, and legible. When the youngster leaves the breeding compartment, pertinent information from the breeding card is entered on the Pigeon Breeding Record (B below). Fill in the breeding card as follows:

(1) PAIR NUMBER. Number of the nest compartment occupied by the parent pigeons.

Pair No. 40

Loft of Pigeon Breeding and Training Center, Camp Crowder, Missouri,

BREEDING CARD

Season, 1944.

Cock No. USA 42 FtM 467 Color B ch
- Sire Soffle-Bastin-Logan
- Dam Osman-Soffle

Hen No. USA 40 FtM 15 Color B ch wft
- Sire Grooter
- Dam Soffle

Date Laid	Hatched	Banded	Band Number of Youngsters		Color, Sex, Remarks
3/2	3/21	3/28	USA 44 SC 1236		B ch C
3/4	3/21	3/28	USA 44 SC 1237		B ch H
4/13	5/2	Destroyed.			
4/15	5/2	Destroyed.			

W. D., S. C., Form 1132   TACK THIS CARD NEAR THE NEST   16— TL 70185

FIGURE 16. PIGEON BREEDING CARD.

(2) LOFT OF. Name of the post, camp, or station where the loft is located, and the designation of the loft.

(3) SEASON. Calendar year.

(4) COCK NUMBER. Date on the leg band that relates to the cock's identification.

(5) COLOR. Color of the cock.

(6) SIRE AND DAM. Strain of each of the cock's parents.

(7) HEN NUMBER, COLOR, SIRE, AND DAM. Data relating to the hen, similar to that furnished on the cock.

(8) DATE LAID. Month and day each egg is laid.

(9) HATCHED. Month and day each egg is hatched.

(10) BANDED. Month and day each youngster is banded.

(11) BAND NUMBER OF YOUNGSTERS. The letters USA, and year of hatching appear in the left column of the band placed on right leg

of youngster. Loft designation and serial number assigned to the youngster appear in the right column of band.

(12) COLOR, SEX, REMARKS. Color of the youngster and remarks, such as disposition when it leaves the breeding compartment. Generally, sex cannot be determined at this time and is entered at a later date.

(13) EGG DISPOSITION. If the egg is removed from its parents to be hatched by other pigeons, or if it is destroyed, its disposition is entered on the card.

B. Pigeon Breeding Record Book, WD SC Form 67 (**fig. 17**). The pigeon breeding record is a PERMANENT record maintained at each loft where breeding activities are conducted. Data are taken from the breeding card of the youngster (see <u>A</u> above) and the breeding record of the parent pigeons, and are entered as follows:

(1) BAND NUMBER. Band numbers assigned to youngsters hatched during the year, in numerical sequence.

(2) COLOR. Opposite the band number, color and sex of each youngster.

(3) NEST NUMBER. Number of the nest occupied by the parent pigeons.

(4) BAND NUMBER, COLOR, SIRE, DAM. Data on each parent, on a separate line.

(5) BAND NUMBER, COLOR, G. SIRE, G. DAM. Data for the parent pigeons (grandparents of the youngsters), entered on separate lines, are obtained from the breeding records of the grandparent birds.

(6) STRAIN. Opposite their band and color, strains of the grandparents of the youngsters.

W. D., Sig. C. Form No. 47

WAR DEPARTMENT
SIGNAL CORPS UNITED STATES ARMY

PIGEON BREEDING RECORD

Band No. −1944−	Color	Nest No.	Band No. / Color (Sire / Dam)	Band No. / Color (G. Sire / G. Dam)	Strain
USA 44 SC 1236	B ch C	40	USA 42 FtM 467 B ch	USA 38 FtM 160 B ch	Soffle-Bastin-Logan
	3/21/44			USA 37 FtM 210 B pd	Osman-Soffle
			USA 40 FtM 15 B ch wft	AU 33 B 1506 R	Grooter
			Winner − 600-mile "Concourse", 1941	IF 37 TOM 124 Dk ch	Soffle
	Races−1944:100; 100 − 3rd; 200 − 1st; 200.				
1237	B ch H		(Nest Mate to No. 1236)		
	Races − 1944; 100; 100 − 4th; 150-1st; 200.				
1238	B ch C	43	USA 41 FtM 121 B ch / 300-mile winner	USA 36 FtM 20 B ch	Ross
				USA 35 FtM 21 B ch	Ross
			USA 39 FtM 280 R	USA 34 FtM 293 R ch	Logan
				AU 36 PGH 26590 B ch	Ross
	Races − 1944: 100; 150 − 3rd.				
1239	B ch H		(Nest Mate to No. 1238)		
	Races − 1944: 100; 150; 300.				

U. S. GOVERNMENT PRINTING OFFICE

TL 70186

FIGURE 17. PIGEON BREEDING RECORD.

(7) NOTES. A small space below each entry, as indicated in figure 16, is used to show:

(A) Date youngster was hatched.

(B) Performance record of the youngster.

(C) Band numbers of any of its outstanding offspring.

(D) Under Sire and Dam, performance record of parent, including maximum flight distance to date, and outstanding racing performance if any.

C. Pigeon Flight Record Book, WD SC Form 1183 (**fig. 18**). The pigeon flight-record book contains flight records of all the birds housed in one loft and is a complete account of their individual performances and training. Each flight made by a pigeon is entered on its record. A flight record is started for each youngster when it is removed from its parents and placed in the flying loft. The record is kept up to date. Entries should be made as follows:

(1) BAND NUMBER. Data on the identification band as shown on the breeding card.

(2) COLOR. Color of the pigeons, also taken from the breeding card.

(3) SEX. If the sex cannot be determined when the form is started, it is entered later.

(4) HATCHED. Date shown on the breeding card.

(5) FLIGHT RECORD. Record of each flight on a separate line under each column as follows:

(A) DATE OF FLIGHT. Month, day, and year the flight was made. Year may be entered at the head of the column to avoid repetition.

(B) Nature of flight. Appropriate description of flight, such as training, signal communication, or race; and how tossed, such as single, double, or group. These abbreviations of entries may be used: Tng, for training; Sig Com, for signal communication; ST, for single-tossed; DT for double-tossed; GT, for group-tossed.

(C) COMPETITION. Number of lofts and the number of pigeons entered in a competition or race.

(D) DISTANCE. Distance traveled in miles (air line) for each flight, and the DIRECTION FROM THE LOFT TO THE POINT OF RELEASE. Abbreviations for directions may be used, for example, NW, SE, etc.

(E) POSITION AND SPEED. Position won in a race or single-tossed training flight (such as first, second) and the speed attained in yards per minutes (YPM) or miles per hour (MPH). Speed is entered for all flights if facts are available for calculation. When birds are group-tossed, enter "late" for those failing to arrive at the loft with the group. If birds break away and arrive at the loft in advance of the group, note position of arrival (such as 1, 2, etc.).

D. Pigeon Pedigree Record, WD SC Form 68 (**fig. 22**). The pigeon pedigree record is kept for each pigeon used for breeding. Data are taken from breeding and other pedigree records, and are entered as follows:

(1) Name, color and sex, registry number (band number), date hatched, by what loft bred, and flight record.

(2) Band numbers and color of parents.

(3) Band number, colors, and strains of grandparents.

(4) In "remarks" include all matters about the pigeon or its strain which bear upon its ability and breeding value.

(5) In the spaces under Father, Mother, Grandfather, and Grandmother, enter appropriate information concerning their flying and breeding records. Pigeon pedigree record, WD SC Form 1177, which is a long form, may be used when necessary if the pedigree is available for the great-grandparents.

PIGEON FLIGHT RECORD   2nd. Sheet

Band No. USA 44 SC 1236 Color ... B ch ... Sex ... C ... Hatched 3/21/44

DATE OF FLIGHT 1944	NATURE OF FLIGHT	COMPETITION		DISTANCE	POSITION AND SPEED	SPEED OF WINNING BIRD	TOTAL DISTANCE, ALL FLIGHTS
		Lofts	Birds				
							234.8
8/12	CT-Tng	2	54	37.3 SW	-	40 M.P.H	272.1
8/13	GT-Tng	2	52	45.3 S	Late	35 M.P.H	317.4
8/15	DT-Tng	1	34	56.0 W	12-50 M.P.H	55 M.P.H	373.4
8/17	ST-Tng	3	76	63.5 SW	5-53M.P.H	60 M.P.H	436.9
8/20	RACE	22	226	90.1 SW	11th to loft-1226 TPM	1335 Y.P.M	527.0
8/23	GT-Tng	1	34	56.0 S	1-35 M.P.H	Group 325MPH	583.0
8/27	RACE	21	230	90.1 SW	3-961Y.P.M	966 Y.P.M	673.1
8/29	Sig Com	1	16	15.0 NE	40 M.P.H	—	688.1
8/31	ST-Tng	2	53	45.3 SW	1-37 M.P.H	—	733.4
9/3	RACE	24	247	186.4 SW	7-1146 Y.P.M	1190 Y.P.M	919.8
9/5	GT-Tng	2	49	28.5 W	—	40 M.P.H	948.3
9/7	Sig Com	1	12	56.0 SW	45 M.P.H.	—	1004.3
9/10	RACE	24	220	196.4 SW	1-1228Y.P.M	—	1190.7

TL 70187

FIGURE 18. PIGEON FLIGHT RECORD.

C. Monthly Pigeon Loft Report, WD SC Form 1133 (figs. 20 and 21). The monthly pigeon loft report is prepared for each pigeon unit on the last day of each month. Blank spaces on the report are filled in as follows:

(1) DATE. Day, month, and year.

(2) ORGANIZATION. Unit submitting report.

(3) STATION. Name of post, camp, or station at which the unit is located.

(4) PIGEONS ON HAND. These notations pertain to birds over 4 weeks of age.

(A) OLD COCKS. Total number of male pigeons over 1 year of age.

(B) OLD HENS. Total number of female pigeons over 1 year of age.

(C) YOUNGSTERS OVER 4 WEEKS OF AGE. Total number of pigeons between 4 weeks and 1 year of age.

(5) AGGREGATE TOTAL. Total number of pigeons, old and young, listed in (4) above.

WAR DEPARTMENT
SIGNAL CORPS UNITED STATES ARMY

PIGEON PEDIGREE

PEDIGREE

Name .... Champ
Color—Sex ... B ch C
Reg. No. .... USA 44 SC 1236
Hatched .... March 21, 1944
Bred By ...... Pigeon Breeding and Training Center, Camp Crowder, Missouri.
Record Raced 100, 100, 200, 200 as young bird winning 3rd, 100, and 1st 200.

FATHER

USA 42 FtM 467 B ch
Reserved for Stock

GRANDFATHER

USA 38 FtM 160 B ch
500-mile "Concourse" winner, 1940
Strain-Soffle-Bastin-Logan

GRANDMOTHER

USA 37 FtM 210 B rd
Reserved for Stock
Strain - Osman-Soffle

REMARKS

Birds of this family have been consistent winners at all distances

Signed .... Otto Meyer
Major, Signal Corps
Date ... Sept. 16, 1944

MOTHER

USA 40 FtM 15 B ch wft
Winner 600-mile "Concourse", 1941
Dam of USA 42 FtM 934 1942 Futurity winner.

GRANDFATHER

AU 33 B 1506 R
600-mile "Concourse" winner, 1936
Strain - Pure Grooter

GRANDMOTHER

If 37 TOM 124 Dk ch
400-mile winner, 1939
Strain - Pure Soffle

Name .... "Champ"   Band No. USA 44 SC 1236   Color—Sex ... B ch C

Form No. 66—W. D. Sg. C.   U. S. GOVERNMENT PRINTING OFFICE 16—34309-1   TL70188

FIGURE 19. PIGEON PEDIGREE RECORD.

(6) AUTHORIZED STRENGTH. Total number of pigeons authorized.

(7) BREEDING ACTIVITIES.

(a) MATED PAIRS. Total number of pairs of parent pigeons mated for breeding purposes.

(b) EGGS. Total number of eggs in nest.

(c) HATCHED. Total number of youngsters under 4 weeks of age.

(8) OTHER PIGEONS. (A) DONATED. Total number of pigeons donated to the Signal Corps by civilian pigeon fanciers.

(B) LOANED. Total number of pigeons loaned to the Signal Corps by civilian pigeon fanciers.

(C) TOTAL. Total number of donated and loaned pigeons on hand.

(9) LOSSES DURING MONTH. (A) DISEASE. Total number of banded pigeons lost or destroyed during the month as a result of disease.

(B) ACCIDENT. Total number of banded pigeons lost during the month as a result of accident.

(C) FLIGHT. Total number of pigeons lost during month while in flight (enter band numbers under remarks).

(D) SALE. Total number of banded pigeons sold as surplus during the month, if any. If none, so state.

W.-D., Sig. C. Form No. 1188
(Revised, 1 January 1944)

"Control Approval Symbol SMT 13"

MONTHLY PIGEON LOFT REPORT

Date 30 June 1944

Organization 300th Signal Pigeon Company Station APO 4210, c/o PM, N.Y., N.Y.
Pigeons on hand: Old cocks 450 Old hens 450 Youngsters over 4 weeks of age 3,500
Aggregate total 4400 Authorized strength 4,500
Breeding activities: Mated pairs 150 Eggs 200 Hatched 100
Other pigeons: Donated 0 Loaned 0 Total 0
Losses during the month: Disease 4 Accident 9 Flight *87 Sale 0 Total 100
Number of birds shipped during month (destination) None

Number of birds received during month (source) 400 young pgns, from lofts at APO 1234, c/o PM, NY, NY.

SUMMARY OF TRAINING

Young pigeons All young birds (over 4 weeks of age) not being used at the front are being trained to mobility for use as replacements. The young birds in use at the front are given exercise flights daily (weather permitting) when not being used for messenger service.

Old pigeons Breeding has been reduced to a minimum since the only requirement is to supply replacements for combat lofts.

INSTRUCTION BY LOFT PERSONNEL

Organization Receiving Instruction	Number Hours	Nature of Instruction
IV Armored Signal Battalion	2	Lecture and demonstration
929th Signal Battalion	2	" " "
77th Infantry Division	10	" " "
8th Motorized Division	10	" " "
7th Armored Division	10	" " "
150th Airborne Division	10	" " "
336th Engineer Construction Battalion	2	" " "

PERSONNEL, ALL OFFICERS AND NONCOMMISSIONED OFFICERS (ASSN 560) OF FIRST THREE GRADES

Army Serial No.	Name and Grade or Rank	Date of Grade or Rank	Date of Birth
0-357145	Capt. Charles B. Still	17 Mar 1944	1 Aug 1914
0-358757	1st Lt. Charles E. Bertin	6 Aug 1942	7 Jan 1910
0-372664	1st Lt. Hersel M. Denoxith	12 May 1943	19 Jan 1913
0-1633633	1st Lt. John A. Hite	16 Nov 1943	1 Jan 1916
0-1637599	1st Lt. George A. Pick	25 Nov 1943	2 Mar 1917
0-1638878	1st Lt. Floyd A. Jones	26 Dec 1943	29 Aug 1911
0-1634895	2nd Lt. Edwin S. Dixon	10 Mar 1943	2 Jul 1916
0-1635792	2nd Lt. Robert B. Holmes	22 Oct 1943	11 Sep 1917
0-1639178	2nd Lt. William M. Bern	30 Nov 1943	1 Jan 1919
43030446	John E. Boson M/Sgt	1 Feb 1942	27 Mar 1914
41003757	George J. Binehan T/Sgt	1 Dec 1942	31 Oct 1913
7146909	Charles H. Wells T/Sgt	17 Feb 1943	18 Aug 1918
42220770	Lawrence Kolic T/Sgt	17 Feb 1943	5 Jun 1919
45040638	John E. Dolan S/Sgt	1 Dec 1942	1 May 1917
49826467	Alfred Trauf S/Sgt	17 Feb 1943	25 Oct 1913
43143724	Bernard Ross S/Sgt	18 Nov 1943	25 Jun 1917

Total Enlisted Strength 149

TL 70189

FIGURE 20. MONTHLY PIGEON LOFT REPORT, FRONT.

(E) TOTAL. Total number of banded pigeons lost during month from all causes listed.

(10) NUMBER OF BIRDS SHIPPED DURING MONTH (destination). Self-explanatory.

(11) NUMBER OF BIRDS RECEIVED DURING MONTH (source). Self-explanatory.

(12) SUMMARY OF TRAINING. Weekly Training Schedules supply information for both classes of birds.

(13) INSTRUCTION BY LOFT PERSONNEL. Organizations receiving instruction, number of hours, and nature of instruction.

(14) PERSONNEL. Self-explanatory.

LOFT EQUIPMENT AND SUPPLIES

Articles	Authorized	On Hand	Requisitioned
Loft PG-46-A (portable)	15	15	0
Loft PG-68/TB	72	72	0
Loft (stationary)	0	0	0
Loft (mobile)	0	0	0
Feed	59,000	20,000	Automatic Monthly
Grit	7,000	2,000	" Issue "
Tobacco stems	300	100	200
Cedar shavings	600	200	400
Quassia chips	300	200	0
Band PG-15 (celluloid)	6,000	6,000	0
Band PG-16 (registration)	6,000 pr	2,000	0
Scraper PG-34-A a/o PG-34	87	87	0
Sieve PG-35	87	72	15
Brush PG-36	87	60	27
Fountain PG-37-C	102	102	0
Pan PG-38 (bath)	87	87	0
Egg PG-40	600	400	200
Crate PG-49 (30-bird)	174	174	0
Cage PG-50 (15-bird)	144	144	0
Message holder PG-67 a/o PG-14	9,000	6,000	3,000
Bowl PG-75	1,200	600	600
Parachute equipment PG-100/CB (4-bird)	144	72	72
Parachute equipment PG-101/CB (8-bird)	144	98	46
Pigeon equipment PG-103/CB (2-bird)	720	500	220
Pigeon equipment PG-105/CB a/o PG-60	720	650	70
Cup, drinking, ½ pt. w/hooks	174	140	24
W. D., S. C. Forms, Blanks:			
No. 67 Pigeon Breeding Record	15	5	10
No. 68 Pigeon Pedigree (short)	1,500	200	1,300
No. 181 Pad, Map Overlay	1,000	300	700
No. 1132 Pigeon Breeding Card	1,000	200	800
No. 1133 Monthly Pigeon Loft Report	200	20	180
No. 1177 Pigeon Pedigree (long)			
No. 1183 Pigeon Flight Record	50	25	25

REMARKS AND RECOMMENDATIONS:

1. See Inclosure No. 1 for band numbers of birds lost in flight or accident and those culled due to disease.
2. See Inclosure No. 2 for complete information on the tactical operation of the company.

*Note: All pigeons lost during the month were lost in training with no birds being lost in tactical operations.

Charles E. Still

CHARLES E. STILL, Capt., Sig. C.,
Commanding

The Commanding Officer will render a consolidated report of all lofts under his command to the Chief Signal Officer, Washington 25, D. C., on the last day of each calendar month in accordance with AR 105–200. This form may also be used to report individual lofts in a command to the Commanding Officer.

When urgent or necessary this form may be reproduced in the field.

TL 70190

FIGURE 21. MONTHLY PIGEON LOFT REPORT, BACK.

(15) LOFT EQUIPMENT AND SUPPLIES. Self-explanatory. Note any item of equipment on hand superseded by an item listed.

(16) REMARKS AND RECOMMENDATIONS. Note information on the tactical operation of the unit; band numbers of birds lost in flight; birds culled during the month (including youngsters), together with the reasons for culling; and any remarks and recommendations not covered

elsewhere on this report. (If additional space is needed, use plain sheets of bond paper.)

(17) COMMANDING. The name, grade, and office of the officer in charge are typewritten or printed in ink below his signature.

28. Banding

A. Each breeding loft is furnished with identifying metal leg bands to be used in banding all youngsters. These bands, PG-16, are manufactured in pairs. Each pair bears the pigeon's serial number.

(1) One of the pair of bands bears a marking which includes U*S, the last two figures of the calendar year the bird was hatched, the letters SC or AAF, and a serial number. This band is placed on the left leg and indicates that the pigeon was bred by the United States Army. It should not be removed as it serves to identify the pigeon with its breeding record.

(2) The other band of the pair bears marking identical to that in (1) above except that in place of the "U*S" it bears the letters "USA." This band is placed on the right leg, and it means that the pigeon was bred by and is the property of the United States Army. This band is removed whenever the pigeon ceases to remain the property of the United States Army.

(3) **Characteristic markings of leg bands now used are as follows:**

(A) Right leg, USA 44 SC 15.

Left leg, U*S 44 SC 15.

(B) Right leg, USA 44 AAF 407.

Left leg, U*S 44 AAF407.

(4) The following designations were used prior to 1944:

FtM.	Fort Monmouth
4CA	4th Corps Area
4th SC	4th Service Command
7th SC	7th Service Command
8CA	8th Corps Area
8th SC	8th Service Command

9th SC	9th Service Command
CZ	Canal Zone
HT	Territory of Hawaii
PI	Philippine Islands
ML	Mobile Loft
C	Combat
PR	Puerto Rico
SC	Signal Corps
TH	Territory of Hawaii

B. In addition to the banded pigeons bred and owned by the United States Army, there are those of the United States Navy, and two large national associations of civilian pigeon fanciers, the American Racing Pigeon Union and the International Federation of American Homing Pigeon Fanciers, as well as those of numerous smaller organizations. The following examples illustrate the character of the legends used on the bands:

USN 32 492AU 28 EC 1245 IF 27 C 6700

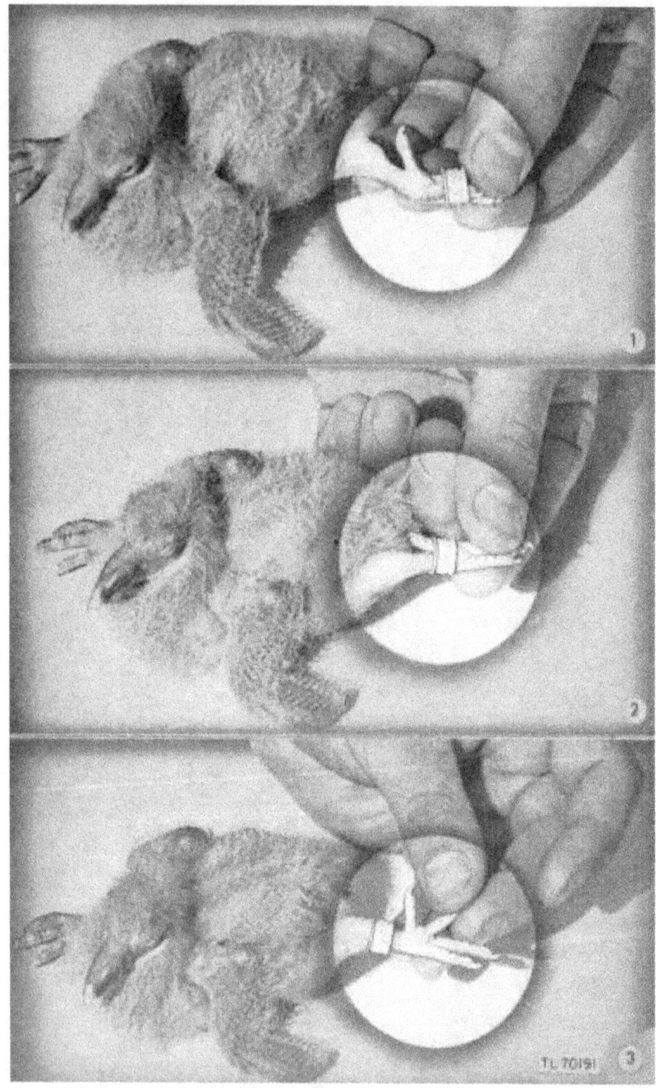

FIGURE 22. METHOD OF BANDING YOUNGSTERS.

C. When banded pigeons are lost in flight, their band markings are listed on the Monthly Pigeon Loft Report (**par. 27 E**).

D. Each loft is authorized to use various colored, spiral, celluloid leg bands for special identification purposes. For example, all pigeons in a particular compartment of each loft may be fitted with celluloid bands of the same color to facilitate keeping track of them. These bands, PG-15, are requisitioned in the following colors: red, yellow, green, light-blue, dark-blue, black, and pink.

29. Loft Equipment

A. T/O & E 11-39 prescribes the authorized allowances of nonexpendable pigeon equipment for signal pigeon companies and is the basis for requisition.

B. Army Service Forces Catalog SIG 4-1, Signal Supply Catalog, Allowances of Expendable Supplies, prescribes the authorized allowances of expendable items for signal pigeon companies and is the basis for requisition.

C. The basis for other pigeon units to requisition equipment and supplies depends upon the number of authorized pigeons they have and their particular needs.

D. Sufficient descriptive information of items must be indicated on the requisition to permit positive identification. All required information pertaining to allowances, supplies on hand, due in (on requisition), and basis for issue must be clearly stated on all requisitions submitted to the station signal property officer.

E. In general, the following items of supplies and equipment in varying numbers will meet normal requirements of pigeon lofts:

Stock No.	Requisition nomenclature	Unit of issue	Brief descriptive nomenclature
9A315	Band PG-15 (Assorted colors)	Ea	Pigeon, leg, marking, celluloid.
9A315B	Band PG-15 (Light blue)	Ea	
9A315BK	Band PG-15 (Black)	Ea	

9A315DB	Band PG-15 (Dark blue)	Ea	NOTE. When specific colors are required applicable stock number should be indicated on the requisition.
9A315G	Band PG-15 (Green)	Ea	
9A315P	Band PG-15 (Pink)	Ea	
9A315R	Band PG-15 (Red)	Ea	
9A315Y	PG-15 (Yellow)		
9A316	Band PG-16	Pr	Pigeon leg, identifying, aluminum; 1 pair to each pigeon.
9A426A	Blow gun	Ea	Blow gun, disinfectant, 1-qt. capacity.
9A575	Bowl PG-75	Ea	Pigeon, pressed wood pulp. Supersedes Bowl PG-29.
9A636	Brush PG-36	Ea	Pigeon loft, counter duster.
9A725	Cage PG-50	Ea	10-bird, training.
9A755	Capsules, multivitamin	Ea	
9A825	Chips, quassia	Lbs	
9A837	Container, 2-bird Fiber board	Ea	Container, assembled 11½ × 6 × 6 in.; dismantled (folded flat) 15 × 12 × ½ in.; net weight, 1 lb.
9A941	Cup, drinking, ½ pt with hooks	Ea	
9A939	Crate PG-49	Ea	20-bird, transportation.
9A1140	Egg PG-40	Ea	Pigeon nest, white glass.
9A1219.2	Feed, pigeon, mixed	Lbs	Feed, pigeon mixture consisting of: 25% Corn, American, small grain; 10% Kaffir; 25% Peas,

			Canada or First and Best; 5% Seed, millet; 20% Vetch, common; 15% Wheat, hard red or durum.
9A1219.4	Feed, pigeon, mixed	Lbs	Feed, pigeon, mixture consisting of: 25% Corn, American, small grain; 25% Peas, Canada or First and Best; 30% Peas, maple; 20% Vetch, common.
9A1219.5	Feed, pigeon, mixed	Lbs	Feed, pigeon, mixture consisting of: 3.5% Buckwheat; 25.0% Corn, American, small grain; 5.0% Kaffir; 2.5% Oats, hulled, table grade; 12.5% Peas, Canada or First and Best; 12.5% Peas, maple; 5.0% Rice, whole, extra fancy; 2.5% Seed, canary; 5.0% Seed, hemp; 5.0% Seed, millet; 15.0% Vetch, common; 6.5% Wheat, hard red or durum.
9A1219.7	Feed, pigeon, mixed	Lbs	Feed, pigeon mixture, consisting of; 10% Corn, American, small grain; 5% Oats, hulled, table grade; 20% Peas, Canada or First and Best; 25% Peas, maple; 5% Seed, hemp; 5% Rice, whole, extra fancy; 20% Vetch, common; 10% wheat, hard red or durum.
9A1219.8	Feed, pigeon, mixed	Lbs	Feed, pigeon, mixture, consisting of: 15% Rice, whole, extra fancy; 20% Seed, canary; 15% Seed, flax;
20% Seed, hemp; 10% Seed, rape, large sweet;			

	20% Seed, millet.		
9A1237C	Fountain PG-37-C	Ea	Drinking, pigeon galvanized iron self-filling, double opening, 1½ gallon capacity, with handle to facilitate carrying. Supersedes fountain PG-37.
9A1321	Grit, health, pigeon (red)	Lbs	
9A1322	Grit, health, pigeon (natural)	Lbs	
9A1646A	Loft PG-46-A	Ea	Portable, 3-section.
9A1648	Loft PG-68/TB	Ea	Portable, combat, transported by ¼-ton Bantam trailer.
9A1767	Message holder PG-67	Ea	Transparent, plastic.
9A1838	Pan PG-38	Ea	Pigeon bath.
9A1845-100	Parachute equipment PG-100/CB	Ea	Pigeon; a collapsible cylinder type container; 4-bird capacity; attached to a 6-ft. parachute with quick release clip.
9A1845-101	Parachute equipment PG-101/CB	Ea	Pigeon, a collapsible cylinder type container; 8-bird capacity; attached to a 9-ft. parachute with a quick release clip.
9A1857-103	Pigeon equipment PG-103/CB	Ea	Complete unit of issue consists of: 1 each, container PG-102/CB (2-bird); 12 each, message holder PG-67; 1 each, map overlay pad Form WD, SC 181; 1 each, message book M-210-A; 2 each, pencils, Black 2H (No. 4) SS-P-186.

9A1857-105	Pigeon equipment PG-105/CB	Ea	Complete unit of issue consists of: 1 each, container PG-104/CB (4-bird); 24 each, message holder PG-67; 1 each, message book M-210-A; 1 each, map overlay pad Form WD, SC 181; 2 each, pencils, black 2H (No. 4) SS-P-186. Supersedes pigeon equipment PG-60, Stock No. 9A1856.
9A1886-106	Pigeon vest PG-106/CB	Ea	Shaped to form a pigeon's body permitting neck, wing tips, tail and feet to protrude, made of porous fabric and has strap for carrying pigeon on paratrooper's or scout's chest, adjustable to any size pigeon.
9A2020	Shavings, cedar	Lbs	
9A2034A	Scraper PG-34-A	Ea	Similar in shape to a putty knife except blade is 3 in. wide. Supersedes scraper PG-34, Stock No. 9A2034.
9A2035	Sieve PG-35	Ea	Pigeon feed.
9A2215	Tobacco stems	Lbs	
6G260.1	Disinfectant	Bottle	Disinfectant, Black Flag (liquid), 1 qt. or equal.
6D67	WD, SC Form 67	Book	Pigeon Breeding Record (long).
6D68	WD, SC Form 68	Ea	Pigeon Pedigree (short).
6D181	WD, SC Form 181	Pad	Map overlay.

6D1132	WD, SC Form 1132	Ea	Pigeon Breeding Card.
6D1133	WD, SC Form 1133	Ea	Monthly Pigeon Report.
6D1177	WD, SC Form 1177	Ea	Pigeon Pedigree (long).
6D1183	WD, SC Form 1183	Book	Pigeon Flight Record.

30. Message Holders

Message Holder PG-67 consists of a body, cap, leg clamp, strap, and fastener (**fig. 23**). The body, cap, and leg clamp are made of transparent plastic material.

A. To attach message holder to pigeon, place leg clamp of holder, around the aluminum identification band on the pigeon's leg and secure strap by means of the fastener. The message holder must always be attached with the cap pointing in the direction of the pigeon's body. If attached with the cap pointing down it will interfere with the bird's walking. The aluminum bands must be loose enough on the pigeon's leg to allow the message holder to adjust itself to positions that will not interfere with the bird's flying. In emergencies, a message holder may be placed on each leg.

B. Pigeons to be used for signal communication should be trained with the message holder attached to the leg to accustom them to carrying it. Pigeons should be distributed to combat troops, with message holders attached if it is known that the receiving troops have not had training or experience in handling the birds. Otherwise, holders may be delivered separately. Personnel of a loft should make every effort to provide message center units being served with necessary information concerning care, handling, and release of birds.

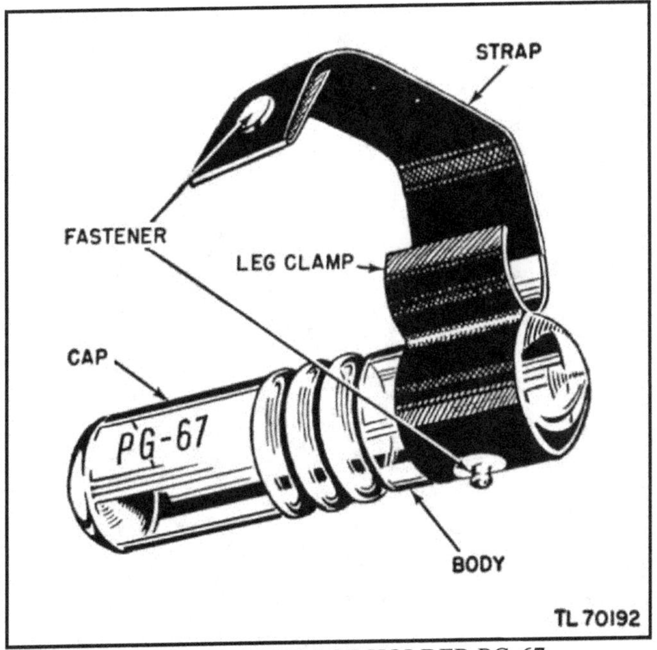

FIGURE 23. MESSAGE HOLDER PG-67.

C. To remove a message from a pigeon, catch the bird after it has trapped; hold it in one hand, extend its leg, and remove the message holder with the other hand. Release pigeon in loft.

D. When it is necessary for a pigeon to carry a message and a message holder is not available, fold message blank, attach it by looping it around the leg band and tie its two ends together with a piece of thread or light weight string.

Caution: NEVER WIND A STRING OR RUBBER BAND AROUND A PIGEON'S LEG because it will stop the circulation and may cause the pigeon to lose its leg.

FIGURE 24. MESSAGE HOLDER ATTACHED TO PIGEON'S LEG.

SECTION V

TRAINING

31. Responsibility for Training

The commanding officer of a signal pigeon company, or the officer in charge of a pigeon unit, will prepare a training program to serve as a general guide for activities of the unit. Weekly training schedules for the guidance of the enlisted personnel will be based upon this approved training program for the unit.

32. Qualifications for Pigeoneers

A. General. Minimum specifications required for a pigeoneer are——

(1) SKILL. That required for a basic private, plus the ability to care for, feed properly, catch, and hold pigeons; to attach messages; and to train birds for messenger service.

(2) KNOWLEDGE. That required for a basic private, plus a thorough knowledge of capabilities, limitations, and habits of homing pigeons.

(3) PERSONAL TRAITS. A pigeoneer who is boisterous and of a turbulent nature tends to frighten and upset pigeons and thus reduce their effectiveness. The successful pigeoneer should possess——

(A) DEPENDABILITY. To perform all his duties regularly and promptly.

(B) KINDNESS. To obtain confidence of the pigeons.

(C) PATIENCE. To spend much time and repeated effort required for training pigeons.

(D) NEATNESS. To maintain a sanitary and attractive loft for the pigeons.

(E) FIRMNESS. To enforce control over pigeons.

(F) POWER OF ACCURATE OBSERVATION. To note and learn characteristics of individual pigeons in the loft by observing details readily and accurately.

B. Basic training. Only qualified basic privates are selected for pigeoneer training. Skill and knowledge to be attained in this course may be based on this manual.

C. Advance training. Qualified pigeoneers who complete basic training prescribed in B above, and who possess the ability, may be selected for advance training which will prepare them to become specialists or non-commissioned officers. This training will teach:

(1) SKILL. (A) Ability to manage a training loft and to train both young and old pigeons.

(B) Ability to manage a breeding loft and supervise breeding activities after schedules have been prepared.

(C) Ability to instruct others in (A) and (B) above.

(2) KNOWLEDGE. A pigeoneer should possess a thorough knowledge of loft management; feeding, training, and breeding of pigeons; and employment of pigeon communications described in this manual.

33. Introduction to Pigeon Training

It is almost impossible to prescribe any one method for training homing pigeons. There are certain steps, however, that must be followed if the birds are to give reliable messenger service. The methods for training Army homing pigeons are prescribed in this section. However, they are not the only methods by which birds can be trained. Success with the birds depends largely on the individual pigeoneer's experience and technical knowledge. This is particularly true concerning operation of combat lofts.

34. Settling Pigeons

Settling is the process of conditioning a pigeon to return to its home loft when released. Best results can be expected from young birds just out of the nest because settling and resettling become more difficult as the age of the pigeon increases. Many different methods are used to settle pigeons to lofts, and no ironclad rules can be set down to cover all situations. The age of the birds, type of loft, and experience of the pigeoneer will determine the method used and success achieved. Two settling procedures will be explained in this section. The first will be for young birds not strong on the wing, and the second for older birds that are strong on the wing. These procedures are general and may be used, with slight variations, to settle birds to all types of lofts. In the case of the combat loft, however, remember that pigeons are trained to recognize a certain type of loft rather than terrain features or geographic locations.

A combat loft is moved daily during training so that the birds do not become accustomed to one location. Otherwise settling to a combat loft is the same as settling to any other loft.

A. Settling birds not strong on wing. The expression "not strong on the wing" means that pigeons do not have sufficient strength in their wings to stay in the air for sustained flight, for example, youngsters removed from the nest when 28 to 36 days old. These young pigeons are tame and easy to handle; they are not as excitable as older birds because their sense of fear has not yet developed. For these reasons they can be easily settled. They are not strong enough on the wing, however, to stay away from the loft for prolonged periods.

(1) FEED AND WATER. Feed birds liberally on the first day they are placed in the loft, but never feed them heavily at any time after that. Make sure the water fountain is placed where it can be found easily. Young pigeons should be kept prisoners for about 2 days. During this time watch them carefully to determine whether all have learned how to drink. If any bird appears sleepy it may not have learned how to drink or where to obtain water. This bird can be taught to drink by forcing its entire beak into the water.

(2) LEARNING TO TRAP. It is of the utmost importance that pigeons used for delivering messages trap promptly. A bird may be the fastest flyer in the loft yet be useless because it will not trap immediately upon return to the loft. The message cannot be removed from the pigeon's leg if the bird stays on the roof of the loft instead of entering the trap. For this reason it is essential that trapping exercises be carefully carried out. The best time for this training is when birds are being settled. Install the trap late in the evening of the second day of confinement and allow the youngsters to go out on their own initiative and look around. This enables them to become familiar with the outside of the loft and the surrounding territory. On the third day catch the youngsters, place them on the landing board, and gently push one at a time through the trap. Some birds may take to the wing but they will only stay in the air a few minutes

at any one time. These pigeons will not fly away; they are merely learning the use of their wings and will return when tired. Place a small amount of feed in the loft during this training and repeat the trapping exercise until the youngsters overcome all fear of the trap. After the birds have learned how to go through the trap allow them to remain outside the loft for about ½ hour and then persuade them to trap into the loft themselves. The birds are especially nervous at this time and should not be frightened. While persuading the birds to enter the loft, the pigeoneer should give them a small amount of feed by hand, and at the same time acquaint them with the feed call.

(3) EXERCISING. On the fourth and following days of training the birds may be turned out morning and late afternoon for approximately ½ hour of exercise. After each exercise period continue training the birds to trap promptly upon their return to the loft. At this time they should be fed only enough to assist in trapping. On these first few days the pigeons may exercise singly or in small groups. On the eighth day or soon after, however, most of the birds will begin to take their exercise flights in one compact flock. As soon as they do this, exercise the birds at noon as this will condition them faster and also accustom them to flying during the heat of the day. If after the seventh day there are a few birds that do not leave the loft for exercise, induce them to fly by pushing them gently off the loft with a bamboo fishing rod or similar pole. After all birds have learned to exercise in a flock for ½ hour or more and then return to the loft they may be considered settled. They are now ready for their first training tosses (**par. 35**).

FIGURE 25. PIGEONS IN TRAP OF LOFT.

B. Settling birds strong on wing. The following method is suggested for settling pigeons that are 36 days of age or older. It is assumed
that these birds have been trained to trap and that they are familiar with the feed call. If they have not been taught to trap, then such training must be carried on in conjunction with this method of settling. It is necessary to use a wire inclosure such as a settling cage in teaching these birds to trap because they will fly away if not confined.

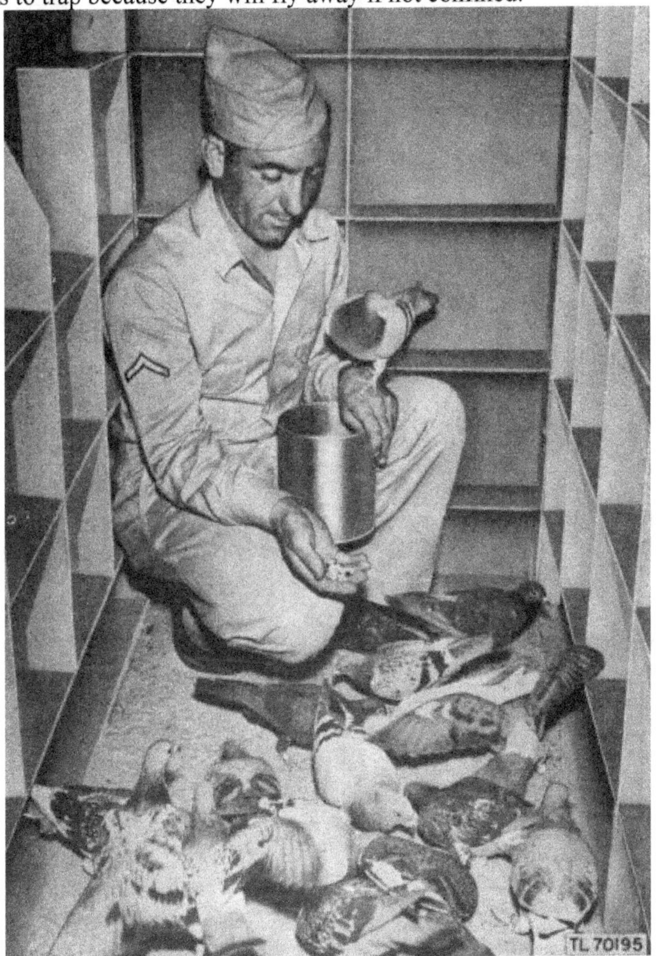

FIGURE 26. HAND-FEEDING PIGEONS IN LOFT.

(1) HUNGER AND TAMENESS. These are the two most important factors in settling birds strong on the wing, and the extent to which they are

developed and controlled will greatly determine the speed with which the pigeons can be settled.

(A) HUNGER. Never feed pigeons a full ration of feed at any one time during the settling period. Keep them definitely on the hungry side at all times. This serves to impress upon them that the loft is the place to find food. Hand-feeding will control the distribution of feed and, at the same time, encourage the birds to become tame. Pigeoneers are urged to hand-feed their birds at all times if possible.

(B) TAMENESS. The pigeoneer should spend as much time as he can in the loft with the birds. The loft should be arranged so that the birds will be near the pigeoneer. This will serve a double purpose: the pigeoneer becomes better acquainted with his birds, and they in turn lose all fear of him.

(2) CONFINEMENT. It may be necessary to confine these birds for several days, depending on their age. A settling cage to fit on the landing board and roof of the loft may be constructed from wood and wire mesh (**fig. 27**). This confines the pigeons, but at the same time allows them to become acquainted with the roof, landing board, trap, and immediate territory around the loft. The qualified pigeoneer can anticipate by the tameness, hunger, and actions of the birds, when they are ready to be given their first freedom.

(3) FIRST FREEDOM. Days with overcast skies or light rains are most favorable for first releasing the birds. Best results can be expected if birds are released in the late afternoon when they are hungry. When the pigeoneer determines that the birds are ready to be given their freedom, or on the third or fourth day of settling at the new location, the following procedure is observed:

Force all of the pigeons into the settling cage, except for three or four birds chosen in advance for their tameness. Give this small group of birds their freedom. Pigeons love company; therefore, after taking to the air, these birds will usually be attracted back by the remaining birds in the settling cage. After the pigeons circle the loft a few times call them in to prevent them from straying. For this first liberation move the settling cage on the loft far enough to one side to expose approximately half of the trap. This permits the pigeons to enter the loft as soon as they return.

When the first group returns satisfactorily, give another small group their freedom. The number of birds in the subsequent groups may be increased if satisfactory results are obtained with the first few groups. If the first group, or any part of it fails to return, however, no other birds should be given their freedom that day. Repeat this procedure the following day.

At no time during the first 2 days of liberty should the entire flock be given its freedom at one time. After approximately 50 percent of the birds has been given their liberty one or more times, the entire flock may be given open loft and permitted to go in and out at will during the late afternoon. Give open loft again the next day at the same time. On subsequent days allow the birds their freedom each morning and evening for approximately ½ hour of exercise.

Any birds that fail to take to the air should be gently forced to exercise. Noon exercise periods will accustom birds to flying in the heat of the day. When all birds have learned to exercise freely in a flock and then return to the loft they are considered settled and ready for further training as message carriers.

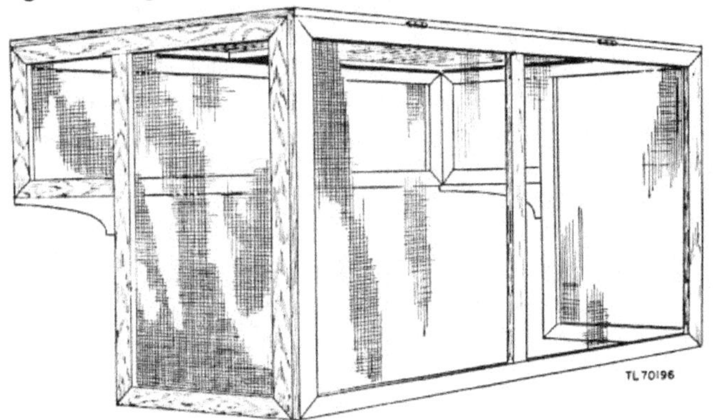

FIGURE 27. SETTLING CAGE FOR LOFT, PG-68/TB.

(4) SUMMARY. These essential points are to be remembered in settling young pigeons:

(A) Teach birds to enter loft immediately after each exercise flight. Loitering outside may become a fixed habit which will make the birds undesirable for messenger service.

(B) Never drive pigeons from the loft during the first few days of settling.

(C) Be sure pigeons are exercised and fed REGULARLY.

(D) Keep birds as tame as possible and do not overfeed them.

(E) At no time allow the birds to become frightened.

(F) Do not interpret these instructions on settling as ironclad rules. It may be necessary to vary them from time to time, depending upon the situation.

35. Training for Messenger Service

This training is started as soon as the birds have been settled to the loft from which they will be distributed. All pigeons except those specifically reserved for breeding purposes may undergo training continuously from the time they are 28 days old until they are no longer suitable for messenger service. Fundamentally, the methods for training pigeons to mobile combat lofts are the same as those for stationary lofts. To avoid confusion, any difference in method will be noted in the following paragraphs.

A. Conditioning. The first step in training homing pigeons for messenger service is to develop the health and strength necessary to endure sustained flight. This process is called conditioning. The degree of training necessary to condition the birds will vary with the mission for which they are being trained. Birds that will be required to fly long distances will necessarily be given longer and more intensive training than birds that will be required to fly only short distances.

(1) HEALTH of the pigeon is dependent on proper care. Overcrowding of birds should be avoided at all times. Good loft sanitation and ventilation, together with proper diet and uncontaminated drinking water, are factors in health that are under the control of the pigeoneer. He is therefore largely responsible for the over-all health of pigeons in his loft.

FIGURE 28. RELEASING PIGEONS FROM CRATE PG-49.

(2) STRENGTH is developed by exercise flights around the loft, and by training flights made from distant points.

B. Training flights. Pigeons may be given training flights in groups, in pairs, or singly. This training procedure is sometimes called "taking the birds down the road for a training toss."

(1) GROUP TOSSING. Three or more birds are released at one time. Young birds are gregarious and will work more satisfactorily when released in small groups rather than individually. For this reason birds being given their first training flights should be group tossed.

(2) DOUBLE TOSSING. A flock of pigeons is released in pairs; each pair is permitted sufficient time to disappear before the next pair is released.

(3) SINGLE TOSSING. One bird at a time is released and permitted to return to the loft alone. This is valuable training and all birds should be given two or more single tosses of 10 or more miles before being used in messenger service. Single tossing should not be practiced at distances in excess of 10 miles until the pigeons have been well settled in a particular location.

(4) USE OF CAGE PG-50 IN TRAINING. Preliminary training of pigeons should include several brief periods of confinement in the 10-bird training cage PG-50. After a period of confinement open doors carefully and allow the birds to emerge of their own free will. The release point should be within sight of the loft.

(5) USE OF PIGEON EQUIPMENT PG-103/CB AND PG-105/CB. Pigeons to be used for carrying messages should be released from these 2- or 4-bird containers after a brief interval of confinement. This will accustom them to the boxes before combat use. Make sure fresh water is available for the birds during confinement period.

FIGURE 29. CAGE PG-50, CONTAINING PIGEONS.

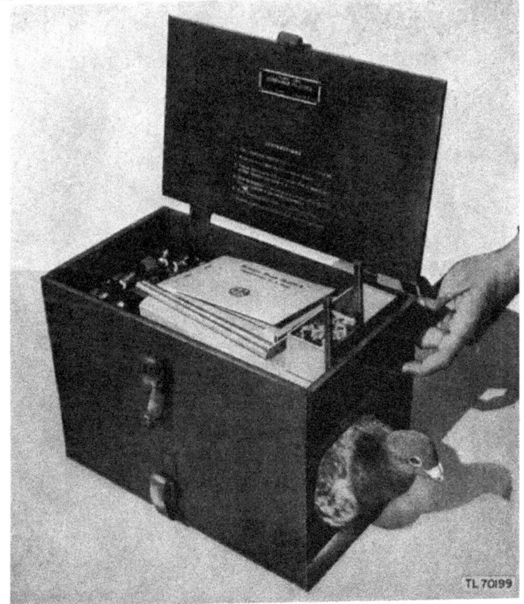

FIGURE 30. RELEASING PIGEONS FROM PIGEON EQUIPMENT
PG-103/CB.

C. Advanced training flights. Advanced training of military pigeons is primarily directional flight training, that is, releasing training pigeons to fly back in one general direction from various distances along the same course. The course may be north, south, east or west as determined by the location of the loft in relation to the point of release. Directional flights are the most suitable for military use, since speed and reliability of the bird are considerably increased and the time involved in training is comparatively short. If properly trained, however, pigeons will return to their loft from reasonable distances in any direction. A return flight from a direction different from the trained line of flight would be called a nondirectional flight. The speed from nondirectional flights will usually be slower and less reliable than from directional flights. This is particularly true when the pigeon must fly from the opposite direction of the trained line of flight. For nondirectional flights to be reliable, pigeons should be given training tosses from varying distances from all points of the compass. Since this type of training is not stressed in the Army Pigeon Service the subject will not be discussed any further.

FIGURE 31. PIGEON EQUIPMENT PG-105/CB, CONTAINING
PIGEONS.

(1) DIRECTIONAL TRAINING TO STATIONARY LOFTS. The
stationary loft training chart (**fig. 32**) will aid the pigeoneer in directional
training of pigeons when the loft is in a permanent location. During
training, flight speeds will average 30 miles an hour from distances of
13 miles or more if a direct line of flight is followed. When the training
flights (**fig. 32**) have been completed, the speed of pigeons will usually
be faster than 37½ miles an hour. To maintain this speed approximately
once a week give pigeons one flight from 40 to 50 miles and two or more
short flights from 15 to 20 miles. Such flights will keep the birds in
condition for messenger service from distances up to 125 miles. Any bird
returning in bad condition will be benefited more by a rest of 3 or more
days than by further training. If birds exceed 40 miles an hour on their
first training flight from release

points of 13 miles or more, they may be failing to observe variations
in topography. Therefore, to be conservative during this training period,

release them again from the same point in order that they may learn thoroughly the physical characteristics of the region over which they fly. This second liberation from the same point greatly assists in avoiding losses at future liberating points from greater distances. A second liberation is also recommended if the birds return at speeds of less than 20 miles an hour, since it can be assumed that they did not follow a direct line of flight. A second flight over the same course gives the birds an opportunity to learn a more direct line of flight. Unless adverse weather conditions exist, pigeons generally continue to fly in a direct line once it is learned. Strong head winds and the need to fly around local storms will slow the birds down.

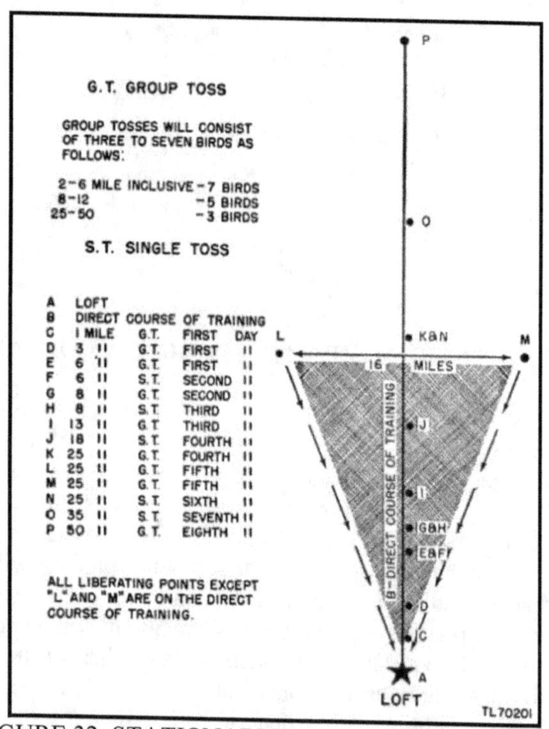

FIGURE 32. STATIONARY LOFT TRAINING CHART.

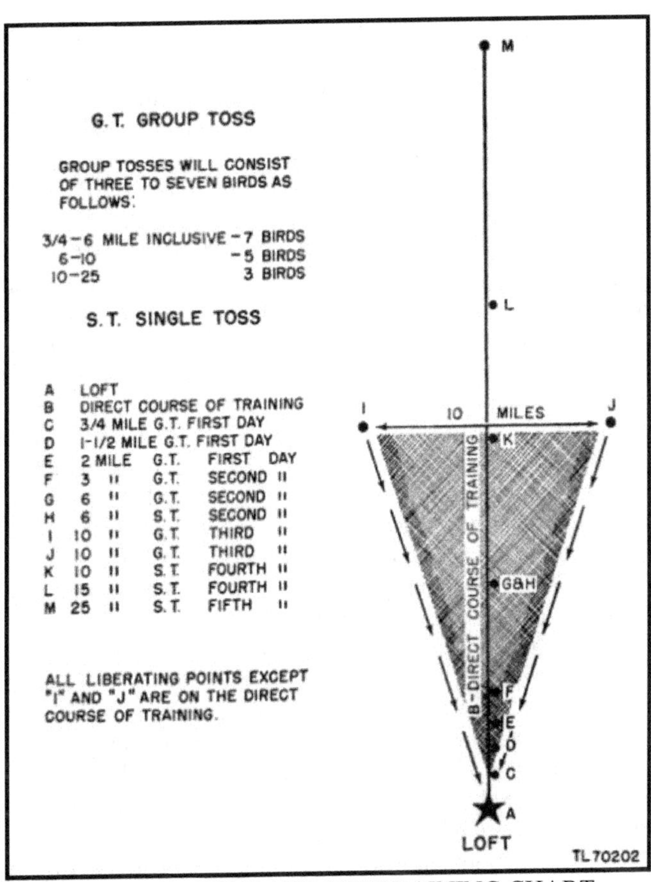

FIGURE 33. COMBAT LOFT TRAINING CHART.

(2) DIRECTIONAL TRAINING TO COMBAT LOFTS. Combat (or mobile) lofts are used during combat when it is necessary to establish immediate pigeon communication. Since pigeons may be required to furnish reliable messenger service within 8 days after moving to a new location, their training must be carefully planned and skillfully accomplished. Flight training begins as soon as the loft is established near the headquarters to be served. Until this time, however, the birds are not given any training tosses. They are, of course, fully settled to the loft and have been taking daily exercise flights around the loft at each new location to which the loft has been moved. Give the birds their first

exercise flight shortly after establishing the new location. After the birds have had a brief rest they are given their first training toss. If weather permits, group toss the birds many times each day thereafter. Increase the distance and reduce the size of

the group each day so that the birds may be trained to distances of 25 to 50 miles in 5 days. When giving this flight training, follow the combat loft training chart shown in figure 36.

D. Remobile training. (1) REMOBILING. After combat birds have been moved into a stationary position and have been flown from this location, it is desirable to train them to mobility again before moving them into a new location. This process is called remobiling and can best be accomplished by moving the loft only a few feet at a time until the pigeons again become accustomed to having it moved. The birds will seem quite nervous and a few may settle on the ground or fail to enter the loft the first few times it is moved. The birds should become accustomed to searching for the loft regardless of its location. After this stage of training has been reached, the loft should be moved farther and farther away from the old location. Work the pigeons as a regular mobile team from this point on, always making sure that the birds are allowed plenty of time in the settling cage before they are released. This process of remobiling homing pigeons can best be accomplished with young birds that have not been settled in one location for more than 6 weeks. If there is a shortage of young birds and it is necessary to use older birds which have been remobiled numerous times, transport them to the new location as many times as possible. Feed the birds at the new location and never at the old home loft. The birds will thus learn to retrace their flight to the new loft if they return to their previous location. This method is useful only when the new location is known in advance. Birds that fail to perform properly as message carriers and are unsuitable for breeding purposes should be destroyed. Birds showing symptoms of sickness should be removed from the loft and forwarded for hospitalization, or destroyed if hospitalization facilities are not available.

(2) REESTABLISHING NEW LOCATION. If the tactical situation requires the message center to be moved forward, a new loft with birds that have been trained in mobility will be placed in the new location. The old loft may continue to operate until the new loft has established reliable communication. This method of operation insures continuous message service. As soon as the new loft has established reliable message service, the old loft will be removed, and if the birds are still suitable for combat

loft flying the loft will be remobiled. If the birds are no longer suitable for combat flying because of numerous resettling at different locations, or from being settled in one location too long, they may be returned to the base camp and put in one of the breeding sections. The combat loft will then be restocked with new youngsters from the breeding lofts and training in mobility will begin.

E. Training precautions. (1) OVERTRAINING. Care should be taken during flight training not to overtrain the birds. Such training does more harm than good, particularly if long distances are involved. Overtraining can be detected by the slightly dizzy, sleepy, and unbalanced appearance of the birds while resting. When this condition occurs, allow the pigeon to rest for a few days with open loft but no forced exercise.

(2) FEED MIXTURES WHILE TRAINING. The birds should have access to fresh water and grit at all times. Make sure that the feed is clean and in the best possible condition. Never change the mixture during training or while the pigeons are being used for messenger service because the change will throw the birds out of condition.

(3) TRAINING LOSSES. Forcing the birds to undertake distant flying before they become properly settled to a location causes frequent losses

during the training stage. Care should be taken to limit the first few training flights to distances of approximately 1 mile or less.

(4) CATCHING PIGEONS. The pigeoneer should avoid quick or sudden movements in the loft and should never chase the birds in order to catch them. When it is necessary to catch pigeons during daylight hours, close the blackout windows or insert the shutters to darken the loft. The pigeons may then be picked up easily with the aid of a flashlight. The pigeoneer should avoid catching the pigeons in the loft immediately after their return from a training flight.

36. Delivering Pigeons by Parachute

A. Equipment. Parachute equipment PG-100/CB consists of a collapsible, cylinder-type, 4-bird container and a 6-foot hemispherical baseball-type parachute with a quick release clip. Parachute equipment PG-101/CB is of similar design except that the container has an 8-bird capacity and is attached to a 9-foot parachute. This equipment is specifically designed to supply initially or to resupply pigeons to infantry parachute troops, infantry glider troops, or any isolated forces requiring delivery of pigeons by air.

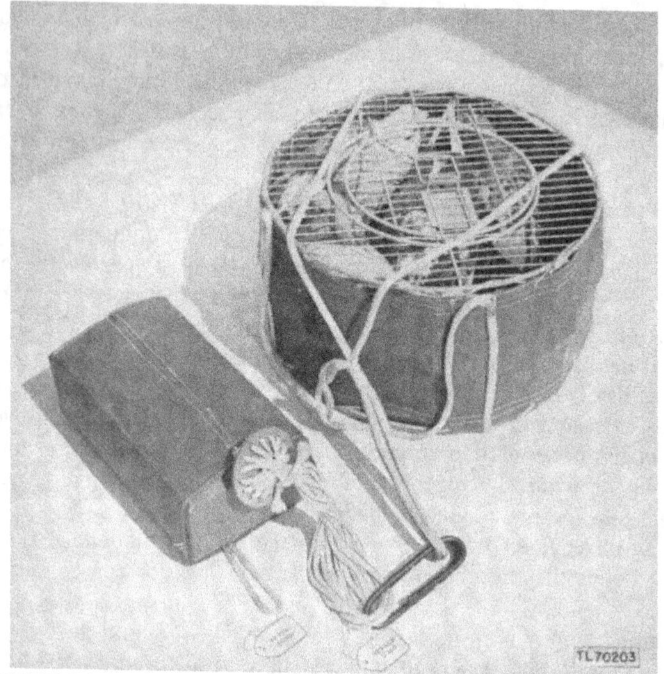

FIGURE 34. FACTORY-PACKED PARACHUTE EQUIPMENT PG-100/CB, CONTAINING PIGEONS.

B. Instructions for use. To insure safe delivery of the pigeons, caution must be observed when attaching containers to the parachutes.

FIGURE 35. PARACHUTE LAID OUT ON FLAT SURFACE.

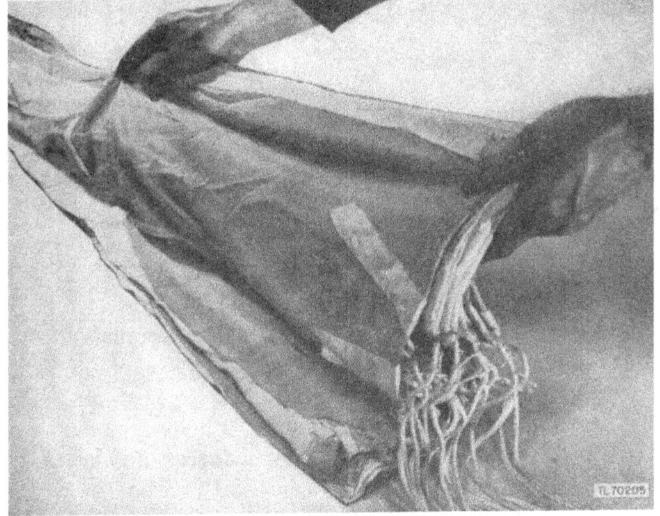

FIGURE 36. PARACHUTE FOLDED LENGTHWISE.

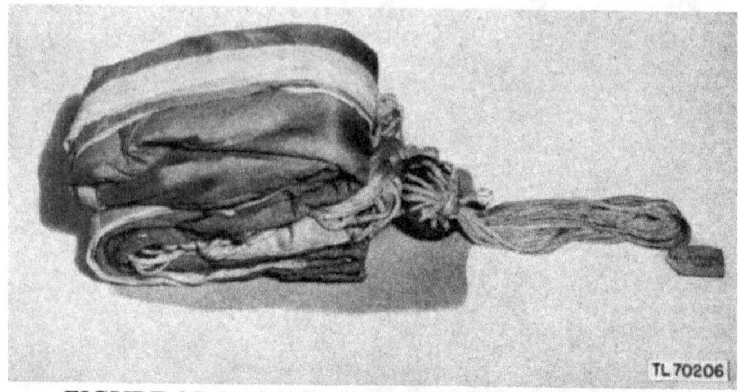

FIGURE 37. PARACHUTE FOLDED INTO PACK.

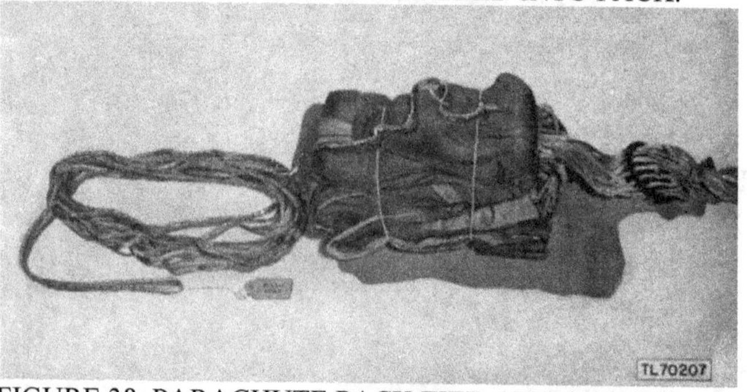

FIGURE 38. PARACHUTE PACK TIED AND STATIC LINE
ATTACHED.

The instructions printed on each parachute pack should be strictly adhered to.

C. Results. Best results will be obtained when pigeons are launched between the altitudes of 200 and 1,000 feet with air speed not exceeding 125 miles an hour. Pigeons launched within these general limits are less likely to become lost because of excessive drift. The possibility of injury to the birds from high speed air rushing through the container, or from shock when the parachute opens, will be reduced to a minimum.

D. Instructions for repacking parachutes. The following method is suggested for repacking either 6- or 9-foot parachutes for future use after they have been used once for dropping pigeons to ground troops.

(1) Stretch parachute full length, with one man holding the canopy at the center of the top and another man holding the shroud lines taut at the shroud line separator disk. Straighten all shroud lines, making sure none

are twisted. Lay the parachute on a flat surface and pick each fold of the canopy as one would pick petals from a flower, dividing the folds and associated shroud lines equally on each side (**fig. 35**). Eliminate creases by running the hand between the folds.

(2) Make an "S" fold in the canopy lengthwise from the crown (**fig. 36**). The hem will form a large letter "S" if the fold is made properly.

(3) Lay the shroud lines in small "S" folds on the canopy starting approximately 10 or 12 inches back from the hem, making a sufficient number of folds to bring the shroud line separator disk close to the hem of the canopy. The parachute is now ready to be folded into a pack. To do this, make three accordion folds in the canopy (**fig. 37**).

(4) Tie the folded canopy in position with two tie cords of not more than 15 pounds strength. Place one cord approximately 2½ inches back from the hem and the other cord 2½ inches from the end of the pack. Attach the static line to the tie cord near the end of the pack, leaving enough tail for another tie to be made to the other tie cord near the hem with 3 inches of slack left between the two ties (**fig. 38**). The static line must have a tensile strength of at least 200 pounds and be 15 feet long. The 3 inches of slack left between the two ties are necessary for each tie cord to receive a sharp individual snap; otherwise both cords will break simultaneously.

(5) Push the remainder of the static cord between one of the folds in the parachute. The parachute is now ready for reuse.

SECTION VI

MATING AND BREEDING

37. Mating

A. General. Pigeons will keep the same mate for life unless forcibly separated. The desire to mate is a natural instinct. Since pigeons are monogamous their mating can be controlled for breeding purposes. If left to their own inclinations, pigeons will mate between the ages of 4 and 9 months. Mating for breeding purposes, however, should not be permitted until pigeons are at least 9 months of age.

B. Purpose. The aim in mating is to produce youngsters which are equal, if not superior, in ability, to either of the parents. Such youngsters are obtained by selecting breeder stock with pedigree, performance, physical qualities, and temperament which will probably produce youngsters of the required type.

38. Sex

A. Sex of the pigeon is difficult to determine without experience; however, some external characteristics help recognition. Under ordinary circumstances the cock usually has—
(1) Broader skull.
(2) Larger head.
(3) Larger bill and wattle.
(4) Stronger neck.
(5) Broader shoulders.
(6) Closer vent bones.
(7) Larger legs and feet.
B. In some cases, where the physical characteristics of the male and female are similar, it is often necessary to observe their actions when together to determine sex. Some of the common actions of the cock are:
(1) Chasing hen when cooing.
(2) Scraping of the tail when cooing.
(3) Pecking the head of the hen when she shows no desire to mate.
(4) Cock's coo is deep and full, while hen's is sharp.

39. Selection of Stock

A. General. Stock for breeding at a loft should be selected with the advice of the pigeon expert in charge of breeding. The pigeoneer who desires to become an expert in the art of breeding pigeons is encouraged to study additional literature on this subject. The pedigree for at least two generations is used to determine probable qualities of future youngsters since it shows family, strain, and kind of flying in which the birds excel, as well as the performance of other youngsters produced by the same parent.

B. Physical qualities. Pigeons selected for breeding should be in good health and as nearly perfect physically as possible. A pigeon which has had a serious injury, or has been very ill, is unsuitable. The following physical qualities are desirable:

(1) FEATHERS. Feathers should be of good quality. Flights, which are most important, should be heavy and wide, and should overlap when the wing is extended, showing no gaps. Birds with very thin flight should not be bred. Body feathers should be soft and plentiful. Those on neck and chest should be glossy and iridescent.

(2) EYE. The eye is complex and is of great importance. It should never be of a sunken or extended nature, but should completely fill the orbit (bone cavity containing the eye) and be surrounded by a fine white textured cere. The eye should be clear and bright; its color is of no importance. The eye may be best examined with a magnifying glass.

(A) The pupil is approximately one-third the size of the eye. It dilates and contracts according to intensity of light and distance of object being focused. The pupil should be black and brilliant.

(B) A thin visible muscle (often called the scouting sight) should completely encircle the pupil. This muscle dilates and contracts the pupil. A portion of the muscle may be of a darker shade and located either at the front or lower front of the pupil. This muscle should be prominent in at least one of the birds selected for breeding to produce a higher percentage of dependable birds. If pigeons which do not possess this muscle, or which have only a small portion of it visible, are to be used for breeding purposes, they should be mated to pigeons having a muscle which is more prominent even though it may not completely surround the pupil.

(C) The iris determines the color of the eye. It should be well blended and possess the brilliance denoting life and observance. Pigeons possessing faded or weak eyes are not desirable for breeding purposes.

Splashed birds often possess a "bull eye" which has an iris of a solid, dark purplish-brown color. When this color appears only on a part of the iris, the bird has a splashed eye. It is hard to detect the muscle surrounding the pupil when the "bull eye" is present.

The color of the iris may be maroon, ruby-red, rose, pink, walnut, chestnut-brown, orange, yellow-orange, carrot, violet, grayish white, or pearl. When the iris consists of one color only, it will be considered a "full eye." Two colors may occasionally be present in the iris, such as red and yellow, orange and yellow, and so forth. The two colors should be well blended in any case. "Full eyes" and "two-colored eyes" are both satisfactory for breeding purposes. Mated birds should have irises of similar shades.

The outer part of the iris is normally darkest; the color diminishes toward the center of the eye. This coloring is more pronounced when the birds are in top condition.

(D) The thin line circumscribing the iris should be extremely dark and very distinct.

(E) The remainder of the eyeball should be dark and well covered by the cere. The bird is said to have an "open eye" when the portion of the eyeball which should be covered by the cere is visible. Birds with open eyes are undesirable for breeding.

(F) The upper and lower lids are a part of the eye cere. A third lid which is a transparent membrane frees the eye from foreign material. The blinking of the third lid can scarcely be detected when the pigeons are in perfect health.

(3) SIZE AND TEMPERAMENT. Medium-sized pigeons are most desirable and birds should be mated to attain this uniform size. Birds being mated
to breed stock for pigeon communication should be calm and easy going, not high-strung. Nervous or excitable birds should never be mated.

40. Line Breeding

The aim of breeding from pigeons of the same or closely related parentage is to reproduce the qualities of the old birds in their young, amplifying the good qualities and minimizing the bad. Line breeding requires the services of an experienced pigeoneer. Only champions which are physically perfect should be mated. Except for line breeding, inbreeding should not be practiced.

41. Nests

A. Bowl PG-75 is an expendable item made of pressed wood pulp and is used as a nesting place for pigeons. It is advisable to replace the bowls occasionally to avoid vermin. Cocks display a keen desire to use the same nest compartment each time they are mated or, if moved to a different loft, the nest compartment in the same relative position as the one occupied previously. If not permitted to do this, the cock will fight the occupant of the compartment. Therefore, consult previous breeding records carefully in assigning nest compartments. Hens do not show this trait, but accept a change in compartments and follow their mates.

B. Keep a supply of tobacco stems for nest material in a rack on the floor of the loft. Allow the pigeons to arrange this material to suit their fancy. Put a handful of sawdust or wood shavings in the nest bowl to prevent breaking of eggs.

42. Control of Breeding

The method of control given below is simple, natural, and successful; it requires minimum handling of the birds.

FIGURE 39. PARENT PIGEONS IN NEST WITH YOUNGSTERS
IN BOWL PG-75.

A. Time. Since best youngsters are obtained when birds are mated during February, March, and April, whenever possible, arrange all breeding for the year during these months. Eggs which should not be hatched should be replaced with EGG PG-50 (glass).

B. Mating. To begin breeding, place each pair to be mated in its nest, and confine for approximately 1 day. Open one of the nests and allow the pair to leave and return at will. The pair may be considered mated after it returns to the nest several times. Close the nest compartment and proceed in the same manner with the next pair, and so on until each pair is mated.

C. After mating. To minimize the danger of birds entering the wrong nest and fighting, open only alternate nest compartments for the first few days after mating.

D. Following season. Any pair producing outstanding youngsters should be mated the same way each year. Mated pairs producing unsatisfactory youngsters should be separated and each pigeon remated. Destroy breeder pigeons which produce unsatisfactory youngsters subsequently.

43. Laying

The first egg is usually laid during late afternoon from 7 to 10 days after nesting has been started. The second egg is laid approximately 44 hours later. As a rule, parent birds do not hover the first egg until the second egg has been laid. This usually enables the youngsters to hatch within 1 hour of each other, and gives each one an equal chance. The youngster from the first egg will be much larger than the other if the parent birds start to hover at the time the first egg is laid. Fertility is indicated if the egg becomes a light bluish color after 10 days, or if it shows blood lines after 5 days when held up to the sun's rays. Do not destroy the first pair of eggs as it is generally believed that they often produce the best youngsters of that year.

44. Hatching and Feeding

A. The incubation period is from 17 to 18 days long. The hen pigeon usually sits from 1600 of one day to 1000 the following morning; the male pigeon sits the remainder of that day.

B. The young pigeons are fed by both parents. Their first feed is a thick, creamy-white excretion produced in the crop of both female and male (pigeon milk or pap). Pigeons are the only birds both sexes of which produce milk for their young. The young pigeon places it's bill down the throat of either parent, and the parent in return forces the food into the young one's throat. This method of feeding is known as "regurgitation."

45. Identification

The identification record of the pigeon is started when the hen lays the egg. Until the time that the youngster leaves the nest compartment, this record is kept on a breeding card (**par. 27**). For identification purposes, each pigeon is banded when approximately 8 days of age (**par. 28**).

46. Culling

It is necessary to cull (destroy) severely to keep the stock in a loft up to standard. Cull birds which do not meet physical requirements for breeding
unless all birds are needed. In addition, destroy those which show a definite lack of intelligence, or which do not perform up to the average. About 30 percent of the young bred in any one season are normally under the physical standard and should be culled to keep the stock from degenerating. In addition to losses sustained through culling, 20 to 30 percent of the remaining stock may be expected to be lost during training flights, as result of disease and injury, or through additional culling because of substandard performance.

SECTION VII

DISEASES AND MEDICINES

47. General

Certain diseases attack pigeons. Normal preventive methods usually protect pigeons from disease. If, however, these diseases are not detected immediately, they are likely to sweep through the loft, destroying or ruining most of the birds. It is necessary, therefore, that the pigeoneer be able to detect, correctly diagnose, and treat the more common pigeon diseases, in addition to taking preventive measures.

48. Prevention of Disease

Disease prevention is much simpler and cheaper than control or cure. Medicines are only emergency measures used in an attempt to overcome disease.

A. Sanitation. This is the most important way of preventing disease and its value should never be underestimated. The following rules for sanitation in the care of pigeons must be strictly adhered to:

(1) Keep loft clean and dry.

(2) Keep drinking fountain clean and water free from pollution.

(3) Quarantine new stock until certain that all birds are free from disease.

(4) Never permit stray pigeons, wild birds, or rodents (mice, rats, etc.) to enter the loft.

(5) Never feed pigeons on a dirty floor, because most of the more serious diseases are transmitted through the droppings.

(6) Bury or burn diseased birds that have been destroyed.

(7) Immediately isolate birds showing any signs of sickness.

(8) After touching diseased birds disinfect the hands before handling other birds.

(9) Thoroughly clean and disinfect lofts contaminated by disease.

B. Loft condition. Pigeons must never be crowded in the loft. It is best to subdivide large lofts into smaller compartments for better control and ease of observation. Sunlight and dryness are two great natural disinfectants which should be utilized fully through plenty of window space and adequate ventilation. Eliminate strong direct drafts because they chill birds and lower their resistance to disease.

49. Control of Disease

A. Pigeons showing any signs of sickness must be segregated immediately. In combat lofts there is normally no place available to isolate and treat diseased birds, therefore, it is usually advisable to destroy them and burn or bury their remains to avoid contaminating the rest of the flock.

B. In any case of disease, the loft should be thoroughly cleaned and disinfected to destroy the germs of the disease as well as the mites and lice which may be carriers. Cresol, saponated solution, is an efficient disinfectant

when used in a 4-percent solution in warm or hot water. This disinfectant is issued to signal pigeon companies.

50. Anatomy and Physiology

A knowledge of the structure and function of the bird's body helps a pigeoneer understand his birds and certain of their diseases. For convenience, the various organs are divided into groups or systems according to their functions.

A. Respiratory system. (1) Mouth and nostrils admit air.

(2) Glottis or larynx is the opening into the trachea.

(3) Trachea conducts air to and from the lungs.

(4) Lungs are organs of gaseous interchange. Air spaces are surrounded by a network of capillaries. Here the blood gives off carbon dioxide and takes on oxygen.

(5) Nine air sacs cool the pigeon, give it buoyance, and mechanically aid the pigeon to breathe.

B. Digestive system. (1) Mouth is the opening through which food is received.

(2) Esophagus conducts food to the crop.

(3) Crop, or ingluvius, stores and softens the food.

(4) True stomach, or proventriculus, furnishes gastric digestive juices that digest proteins and carbohydrates.

(5) Gizzard is the grinding and mixing organ.

(6) Pancreas furnishes digestive juices that digest fats, proteins, and carbohydrates, besides furnishing certain internal secretions.

(7) Liver produces bile which helps digest food.

FIGURE 40. LOFT CLEANING EQUIPMENT.

(8) Intestines provide space for food while it is being digested and absorbed by the blood stream. The intestines also furnish some digestive juices.

C. Circulatory system. The circulatory system consists of the heart, arteries, veins, and capillaries. Its function is to convey nourishing blood from the heart to all parts of the body and to dispose of the waste material produced by the working tissues. The heart consists of four chambers: two ventricles and two auricles. The right auricle receives the stale blood from the veins and pumps it into the right ventricle which pumps it through an artery to the lungs. Here waste matter, such as carbon dioxide, is eliminated from the blood and fresh oxygen is restored. The blood then returns to the heart through a vein entering the left auricle. Proceeding from the left auricle to the left ventricle, it is pumped out through the arteries to the capillaries, which are the smallest vessels of the body. The capillaries circulate the blood through every tissue of the body, dispensing oxygen and food. The blood then picks up waste material on its return to the heart through the veins. The circulation of blood in the pigeon is very rapid, and with the heart beating 200 to 300 times a minute, only a few minutes are required to complete the circuit.

D. Reproductive system. (1) Male birds have two testes (testicles).

(2) Female birds have one (left) ovary and one oviduct, or egg tube, through which the yolks pass to get the albumin, shell membrane, and shell.

E. Urinary system. The kidneys take impurities out of the blood, and pass them into the cloaca (combination bladder and rectum).

51. Indications of Sickness

A. The common indications of sickness are—
(1) Refusing to eat.
(2) Dull, watery eyes.
(3) Droopy appearance with ruffled feathers and no desire to move.
(4) Green, watery droppings. If such droppings are noted in the loft all birds should be watched until the sick one is detected.

B. The easiest and best way to detect sick pigeons is to observe the birds at feeding time. The pigeoneer should also examine all birds as they are being basketed for training tosses.

52. Diseases

Pigeons are subject to numerous infectious and contagious diseases. These diseases are caused by germs such as bacteria and viruses, and are transmitted in poor feed, dirty water, unclean lofts, and similar conditions showing mismanagement. Infectious diseases are contagious if the birds themselves transmit germs to one another.

A. PIGEON POX is a common infectious, contagious disease which usually affects unfeathered portions of the pigeon's head and feet. Pox often develop on the mucous membrane, lining of the mouth and throat. In an outbreak, both types are usually seen. The pox appear as swellings covered with light yellow material and are sometimes called wet pock, diphtheria, or canker.

(1) SYMPTOMS. The course of the disease runs about 4 weeks.

(A) The virus gets into the skin or mucous membrane and causes a wartlike swelling, called a pock, at the point of infection. The virus grows and causes the pock to enlarge for about 10 days.

(B) During the next 10 days the tissues begin to die and turn yellow.

Sometimes a blister forms in the pock, but only a slight enlargement occurs during this period. During the last 10 days the affected tissues begin to dry and form scabs which soon heal and drop off.

(C) Pock in the mouth and throat follows the same course as in (B) above except they are covered with a light yellow layer of tissues. Instead of becoming a dry scab formation, the pock becomes a yellow cheesy formation.

(2) TREATMENT. Usually this is of little value, as pox will run its course of about 4 weeks, regardless of treatment.

(A) One percent yellow oxide of mercury ointment will help soothe affected eyes.

(B) Pock in the mouth may be cut away, and the area painted with tincture of iodine or carefully cauterized with silver nitrate to stop bleeding.

(C) Birds that refuse to eat may be fed by force until the disease runs its course.

(D) Vaccination has no curative value on affected birds.

(E) Thoroughly clean and disinfect loft after an outbreak of this disease.

(3) PREVENTION. This is simple if all susceptible birds are vaccinated. Vaccination against pox is one of the most successful known because all birds receiving it are made permanently immune. Birds may be vaccinated at 5 or 6 weeks of age.

(A) Pluck five or six feathers from the breast region of the bird and brush the vaccine into the follicles.

(B) In about 10 days the follicles swell and a pock develops. This runs a course of about 4 weeks and heals.

(C) All susceptible birds in a loft should be vaccinated at the same time and each should be examined for "takes" after vaccinations.

B. Paratyphoid is a common infectious disease of pigeons and is probably the most devastating of bacterial infectious diseases at the present time. It may affect the bird in many ways, and produce such a variety of symptoms that it is often mistaken for numerous other diseases. The only definite way of diagnosing paratyphoid is by laboratory tests. A tentative diagnosis can be made, however, upon observing typical symptoms.

(1) SYMPTOMS. The course of the disease varies from a rapidly fatal blood poisoning to a slow, chronic disease with, or without, complete recovery. The infection may take place through the egg, by way of milk fed to youngsters, or by contaminated feed, water, and grit. The manner of infection has no bearing on the course of the disease. The germs may get into the blood-stream, go all through the body, and cause

sudden death; or the infection may be less severe and localize in any one of the numerous organs.

(A) Bacteria may localize in the intestines and produce mild to very severe inflammation. This usually results in diarrhea.

(B) Localizations in the lungs are very common and appear as hard, dried abscesses. These are seldom so serious as to cause respiratory distress.

(C) Joint boils result from direct localization of the germs in the joints of the legs or wings. Naturally this produces lameness.

(D) Inflammatory reactions of the spleen and liver are often the result of the localization of the germ in these organs. Chronic inflammation of the entire liver is also observed. The abdomen of such birds usually fills with fluid and the bird then gets thin and dies.

(E) Paratyphoid germs quite often localize in the brain and cause abscess formation. Such abscesses cause a variety of symptoms, depending on which part of the brain is involved. Usually the bird shows loss of equilibrium. It may twist its head and neck about, show trembling of the head and neck, or other nervous symptoms. Such birds rarely recover.

(F) Occasionally the germ will localize in the eye. The inside of the eye turns white and sight is lost. Only rarely are both eyes involved. Such birds appear to be very ill and usually die in a short period of time.

(G) Germs may localize in the ovary of the female or testes of the male. Such birds may show no symptoms, or they may become sterile. Eggs laid by such birds may be infertile. Youngsters, if hatched, may be weak and die soon after. Germs may localize in the oviduct and cause an impacted oviduct.

(H) The only definite way of diagnosing paratyphoid is by laboratory tests. A tentative diagnosis can be made, however, upon observing the typical symptoms.

(2) TREATMENT. Treatment is useless for visibly affected birds. Neither drugs nor vaccines seem to be of any value in treating this condition. Many birds recover from mild infections without treatment. Therefore, the best possible care should be provided for the birds in order to keep their resistance high so that they can successfully combat the infection and overcome disease.

(3) PREVENTION. Since contamination of feed, water, and grit by droppings is probably the greatest cause of paratyphoid, sanitation is the best preventive.

(A) Clean the loft scrupulously.

(B) Maintain sanitary drinking fountains with fresh water to avoid spreading infection by way of water. Take special care to prevent dampness from spillage or leakage around the drinking fountain, as this makes an ideal place for bacteria to accumulate.

(C) Feces from birds with diarrhea should be removed from the loft as soon as noticed.

(D) Frequent disinfection of the loft with a strong disinfectant like 4 percent saponified cresol will help keep down contamination.

C. Trichomoniasis. This is a very common disease of pigeons commonly seen in the mouth, esophagus, or crop in the form of cheesy yellow or white lesions. For this reason it is often called "canker" by pigeon fanciers. The cause is a motile one-celled organism. Only the common type of this organism will be considered here. This disease has many carriers. It shows up only where sanitary conditions are bad or other diseases are present.

(1) SYMPTOMS. The course of the disease varies according to resistance of the affected bird, treatment, and care. Young birds in the nest become infected through "milk" of infected parents. Infection doubtless spreads by contact while "billing" and fighting. Germs cause affected tissues to die. This results in the formation of a sore or opening down into the tissue with a varying-sized yellow, cheesy exudate or scab forming over it. Sometimes such scabs become very large and nearly fill the mouth, throat, or crop.

(2) TREATMENT. Various drugs and chemicals have been used to treat trichomoniasis. However, this condition has proved quite unresponsive to usual medication. In fact, drugs do not have much, if any, direct effect on the healing of tissue. All that medicine can do is to cut down the number

of parasites present and permit nature to repair the damage done to the tissue. Suggested procedures for treatment follow:

(A) Remove all yellow pus patches with cotton swabs. Then paint area with a mixture of iodized oil and sulfanilamide powder. The iodized oil is prepared by using 1 gram iodine, 1.5 grams potassium iodide, and 2 ounces light petrolatum. The iodine requires some time and frequent shaking to dissolve. Make a small cotton swab on an applicator stick, dip it into the oil, roll it in the sulfanilamide powder, and then apply to cleaned trichomoniasis (canker) lesion. Daily treatment, rest, and an abundance of good feed are necessary.

(B) Clean off exudate by local applications of tincture of iodine, or a mixture of one part iodine to three parts glycerine; at the same time lesions will respond to such treatment. Silver nitrate may be used either in stick form or in solution.

(3) PREVENTION. Sanitation is the best preventive.

(A) Correct predisposing causes such as wet floors, nests, and perches.

(B) Try to isolate infected birds, provided the number is not too large.

(C) Attempt to control spread of parasitic infestation by using a parasiticide like copper sulphate in the drinking water. This is used in a 1-2000 solution.

D. Tuberculosis. This is an infectious and highly contagious disease caused by a highly-resistant germ which can live in soil for 2 years.

(1) SYMPTOMS. The young die suddenly and old birds waste away. Grayish white nodules appear in liver and spleen, basket ulcers in intestines, and yellow nodules in all parts of the body.

(2) TREATMENT. There is no treatment for tuberculosis. Destroy all affected birds and thoroughly clean and disinfect loft.

(3) PREVENTION. Keep all stray pigeons out of loft and maintain sanitary conditions at all times.

E. One-eye cold (CONJUNCTIVITUS). (1) SYMPTOMS. There is a watery discharge from the eye, and the surrounding membranes are frequently swollen.

(2) TREATMENT. Place bird in a warm room and treat eye daily with one drop of metaphin, or one drop of 15 percent argyrol.

(3) PREVENTION. Provide proper ventilation in the loft. Avoid dampness and drafts.

F. Going light. This is not a disease in itself but a symptom or result of a disease. Any pigeon showing loss of flesh should be isolated and observed until the affecting disease is determined.

G. Diarrhea. This is not usually a distinct disease, but the result of some other disease.

(1) SYMPTOMS. Droppings are green and watery.

(2) TREATMENT. Sick birds should be isolated and observed to determine if they have some other disease. Feeding of rice will usually check the condition if it is caused by feed or drinking water.

(3) PREVENTION. Sanitary loft conditions, proper diet, and fresh drinking water will help prevent it.

H. Sour crop. Sour crop is caused by damp or mouldy grain, impure water or lack of grit.

(1) SYMPTOMS. The pigeon will sit with feathers ruffled. A greenish diarrhea usually accompanies sour crop. On examination the crop is found to be hard and distended.

(2) TREATMENT. Hold the bird with head down and gently press on the crop until all feed has been removed. Flush out the crop with a solution

of 4 teaspoons of bicarbonate of soda to a quart of warm water. Feed a light mixture, consisting mostly of rice, millet, kaffir corn, and other small seeds. Repeat the cleaning and flushing of the crop daily, if necessary, until this condition clears.

(3) PREVENTION. Sanitary loft conditions, proper diet, and fresh drinking water will help prevent it.

53. External Parasites

Many insects and related species live off other animals. Some of these parasites, like lice, live on the host but feed only upon bits of its feathers and tiny scales and excretions of the skin. Others are more vicious and suck blood from the animal. Diseases are often spread from bird to bird through the life habits of these parasites.

A. Lice. Lice are undoubtedly the most common of these external parasites.

(1) DIFFERENT SPECIES. There are at least six different species of lice that attack pigeons in this country. The three most common are—

(A) FEATHER LOUSE. This is the long, slender species that lives on the barbs and shaft of the feather over nearly any part of the bird's body.

(B) GOLDEN FEATHER LOUSE. This louse is a little shorter and much broader and lives on the feathers, particularly on the bird's body.

(C) BODY LOUSE. This is the largest of the pigeon lice. It lives on the skin rather than on the feathers. It is thought that these lice, by biting the very young pin feathers when they are filled with blood, cause the small pinhole perforations often seen in pigeon feathers.

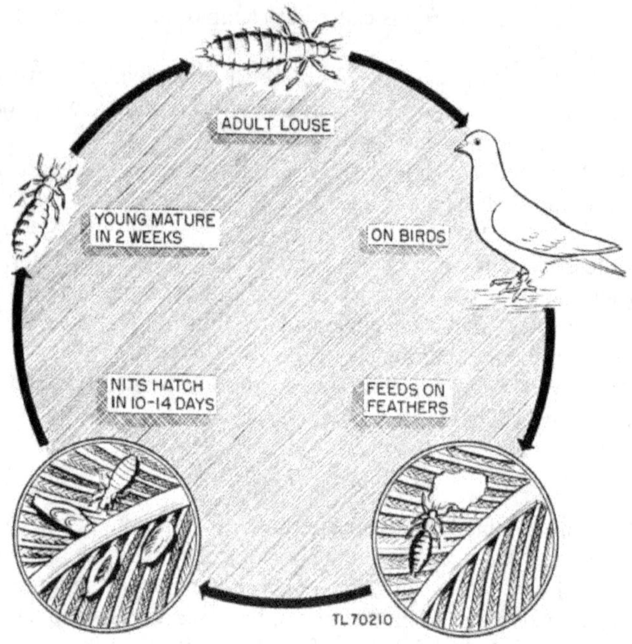

FIGURE 41. LIFE CYCLE OF PIGEON LICE.

(2) HABITS (**fig. 41**). In order to combat lice properly and intelligently, it is necessary to know something about where and how they feed, live, and breed.

(A) Adult lice live on the skin and feathers of the bird and only rarely leave the pigeon. When accidentally dislodged, they crawl very short distances to other birds. Lice cannot live longer than a few days away from the birds.

(B) Lice eat bits of feathers, scales, and other debris off the skin. They do not suck blood.

(C) Female lice lay eggs (nits) along the shafts of the feathers, particularly on the primary coverts.

(D) Louse eggs hatch in 10 to 14 days.

(E) Young lice eat, molt (3 to 5 times), and grow to maturity in about 14 days.

(3) DIAGNOSIS. Infested pigeons are restless and constantly pick and scratch in an effort to dislodge the lice. Heavily infested birds may become weak and thin because the constant annoying movement of lice

interferes with their proper relaxation and rest. Careful examination of the birds will reveal the lice.

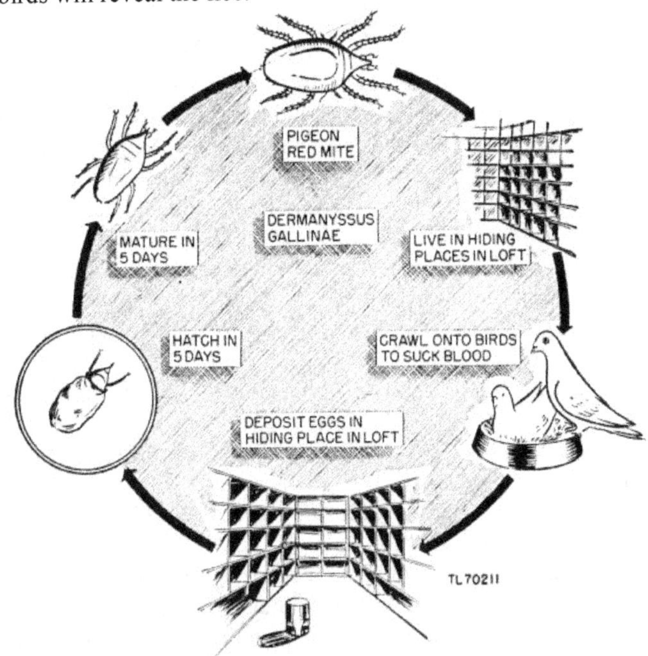

FIGURE 42. LIFE CYCLE OF COMMON RED MITE.

(4) TREATMENT. The use of sodium fluoride is a good standard method for ridding pigeons of lice. It can be applied in two ways:

(A) DIP METHOD is very efficient, but can be used only in warm weather. Birds should be dipped on a warm, sunny day early enough so they will dry before night. Each bird is immersed into the solution up to the head, and the feathers ruffled to allow penetration of the solution. Then the mouth and nostrils are held shut and the head immersed. The dip is made of 1 gallon warm water, and 1 ounce sodium fluoride.

(B) DUST METHOD may be used at any time. The birds are held while a few pinches of powdered sodium fluoride are dusted into the feathers over various parts of the body. Sodium fluoride poisons lice when they eat it. Efficiency in delousing birds depends on thoroughness of wetting or dusting.

(5) REPEAT TREATMENT. Neither method above will kill nits nor prevent them from hatching; therefore, the delousing must be repeated in 10 to 14 days in order to kill newly hatched lice.

(6) PREVENTION. Normally, only pigeons carry pigeon lice. For this reason, the spread of lice to or from other kinds of birds is of no concern. However, common pigeons and stragglers are prolific sources of spread. Contact in crates is also a common source of infestation. Lice are often brushed from infested birds onto the hands and clothing of pigeoneers who later carry them to clean birds handled later.

B. Red mites. Red mites are a common parasite of the pigeon.

(1) HABITS (**fig. 42**). It is important to note the difference between the habits of lice and mites.

(A) Mites live in, on, and under the nest bowls, nest boxes, and any available crack or crevice.

(B) Mites go onto the birds only long enough to feed—usually about ½ hour.

(C) Red mites suck blood from the pigeons. It is the engorged blood that makes the mite red.

(D) Mite eggs are deposited in the cracks and crevices or debris around the nest box where they live.

(E) Eggs hatch in 2 or more days, according to weather conditions.

(F) Newly-hatched mites mature in about 5 days.

(2) DIAGNOSIS. Pigeon's loss of condition is the most evident indication of mite infestation. Actual loss of blood is probably less harmful to the bird than annoyance caused by crawling and biting of mites.

(3) TREATMENT. Most good disinfectants supplied to lofts will kill mites satisfactorily if worked well into all cracks and crevices. Oily disinfectants are inexpensive and very effective, but leave the loft rather unsightly. Whitewash kills only by covering up and is ineffective if any areas are missed. For this reason, some of the more refined cresols are used. Four percent saponified cresol in warm water is quite effective.

(4) REPEAT. Since the cresol does not kill the eggs, it is necessary to repeat treatment in 5 to 7 days.

(5) PREVENTION. Mites that attack pigeons are apparently the same as found on other birds, including domestic poultry. Therefore, wild birds, straggling pigeons, and neighborhood poultry are possible sources of infection. Light, dry, airy lofts do not favor breeding of mites.

C. Pigeon flies which are particularly troublesome in warm climates are true flies with short, flat, wide bodies and long wings.

(1) LIFE CYCLE (**fig. 46**). (A) Pigeon flies live among body feathers.

(B) They leave the birds only to deposit larvae, or when disturbed.

(C) Adult flies suck blood from the birds.

(D) Female flies deposit living larvae in or around the nest bowl, nest box, or around the loft.

(E) Newly deposited larvae are white and about the size of a small buck shot. Within a few hours, a hard shell forms around them and they turn from white to brown and then to jet black.

(F) Young flies emerge from these shells in about 30 days and are ready for their first meal of blood.

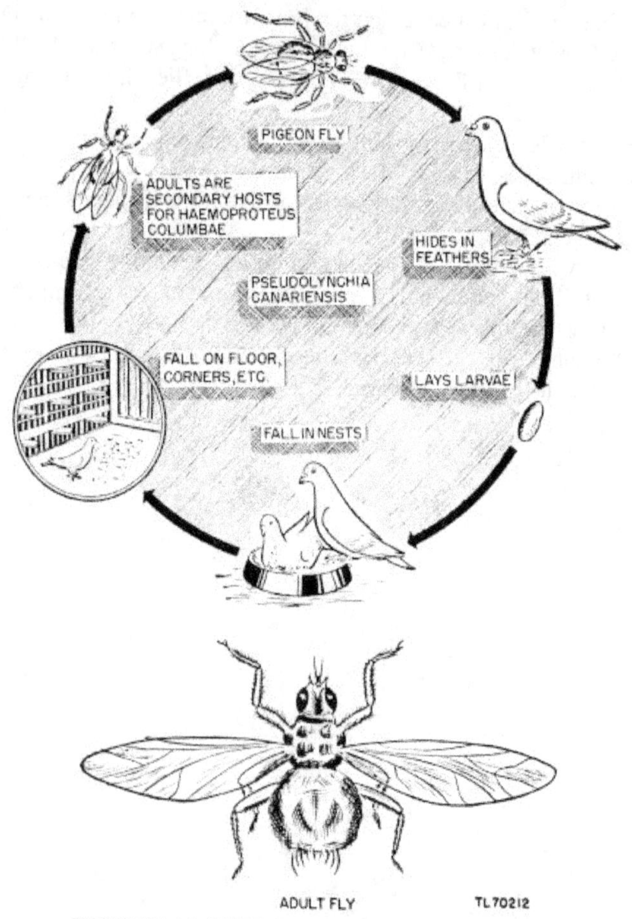

FIGURE 43. LIFE CYCLE OF PIGEON FLY.

(2) DIAGNOSIS. Pigeon flies can easily be observed crawling among the
bird's feathers. Their movement as well as biting greatly annoys the birds. However, the greatest damage they do is transmitting pigeon malaria.

(3) TREATMENT. A very effective and easily applied method of treatment is to dust the birds lightly with pyrethrum powder. Sweep nest boxes and loft carefully to collect pupae so that they can be destroyed.

Pigeon flies will not travel far from the birds; therefore, keep stragglers out of loft and carefully inspect newly-introduced birds to avoid admitting flies.

D. Mosquitoes. Mosquitoes are a very common but usually underestimated pest. Besides molesting the birds by biting and sucking blood, they may transmit pox. These troublesome insects breed in standing water, such as swampy areas, old tin cans, and rain barrels. Control consists of draining or oiling breeding places and using screens on loft openings.

E. Other parasites attacking pigeons are fleas, chiggers, ticks, bed bugs, depluming mites, feather mites, air sac mites, subcutaneous mites, sand flies, and beetle larvae. Fortunately, these are rare.

54. Internal Parasites

These are the worms that live inside pigeons. Round worms are by far the most numerous. Tape worms are occasionally found in pigeons, but seldom present a serious problem.

A. Ascarids, or common large round worms are the largest and most prevalent of the round worms. Adult worms are from 1 to 2 inches long.

(1) HABITS. Knowledge of the life cycle of a round worm is of great importance for successful control of this troublesome parasite. This worm has a "direct" life cycle (**fig. 47**) (completing it in one species).

(A) Mature worms live in the upper part of the small intestines and feed by absorbing food from the intestinal contents through their own body walls.

(B) Eggs (ova) are deposited by female worms in the intestinal contents of the pigeon, and later pass out in the pigeon droppings. It has been estimated that female worms lay as many as 12,000 eggs a day. Feces from parasitized birds often contain countless numbers of ova.

(C) Freshly deposited worm eggs are much like freshly laid pigeon eggs, in that they must be incubated before they are ready to hatch. They need to remain in warm, moist litter or soil for 10 to 16 days before the worm larvae can develop. Severe freezing, excessively hot soil, and direct sunlight will destroy the eggs.

(D) When birds eat the incubated eggs, the worms hatch out in their intestines.

(E) The tiny larvae then "sew" themselves into the lining of the intestines and begin to grow.

(F) After a few days, the larvae crawl back into the intestinal canal where they mature in 30 to 40 days.

(2) DIAGNOSIS. Ascarids injure birds in several ways.

(A) When the newly hatched worm "sews" itself into the intestinal lining the area around the puncture becomes inflamed because of mechanical injury, loss of blood, and introduced infection. This localized inflammation renders that part of the intestinal lining useless for digesting and absorbing food.

(B) The worm absorbs food from the intestinal contents which should go to the birds.

(C) In order to protect themselves and avoid being digested, the worms give off a substance that neutralizes digestive juices. This substance becomes mixed with intestinal contents and prevents proper digestion.

(D) Worms sometimes become so numerous that they actually clog the intestines. As many as 500 worms have been found in a single bird.

(E) Worm-infested birds show loss of condition and general unhealthiness. Diagnosis is made by finding worms or worm eggs in droppings or by autopsy on typical specimens.

(3) TREATMENT. The following drugs are only effective against mature worms and, at best, are only 80 percent efficient:

1-CC Oil of turpentine per bird.

½-CC Tetrachlorethylene per bird.

½-CC Carbon tetrachloride per bird.

(4) PREVENTION. This is relatively simple and practically 100 percent effective.

(A) Clean loft daily and provide fresh water.

(B) If aviary does not have a wire bottom spread clean sand about 1 or 2 inches deep over its floor once every two weeks.

(C) Replace moisture and shade by sunshine and dry conditions.

B. Strongyles are the most dangerous of the common round worms and one of the most common causes of death among poorly kept pigeons. The "strongyle" is a very small parasite which multiplies rapidly and is a vicious blood sucker. Adult worms are from ½ to ¾ inches long and about the same size as thin thread.

(1) HABITS. This worm has a "direct" cycle; that gives the key to successful control (**fig. 45**).

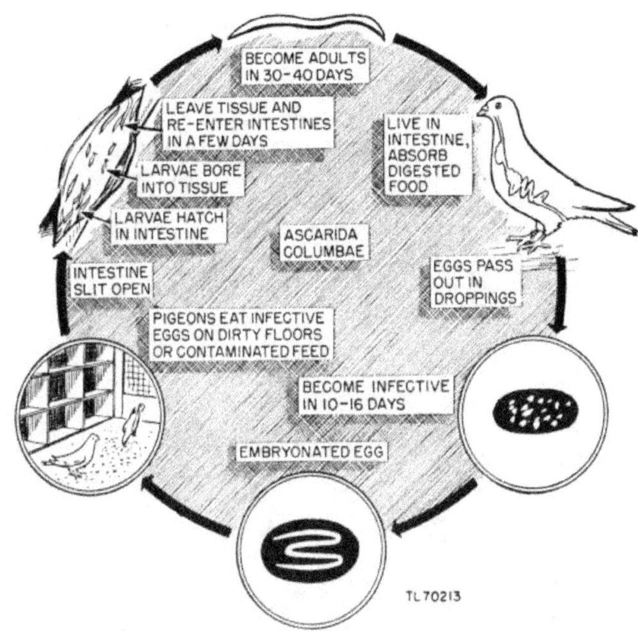

FIGURE 44. LIFE CYCLE OF PIGEON ASCARIDS.

(A) Adult strongyles live in the upper intestinal contents, but may be found as far up as the crop.

(B) Strongyles are ravenous blood suckers.

(C) Female worms deposit eggs in the intestinal contents which later pass out in the feces.

(D) Eggs incubate in about 1 day, if conditions are favorable.

(E) Young larvae hatch out and molt about 8 hours later. These larvae again molt in about 3 days and are then infective. Thus, about 5 days elapse from the time the eggs are voided by the bird and the time the young larval worms hatch, molt, and become infective.

(F) The infective larvae are eaten by the pigeons. Then they pass to the intestines where they mature.

(2) DIAGNOSIS. (A) Strongyles injure the birds by lacerating the intestine and sucking blood. After the parasite moves on, the laceration still bleeds considerably before a blood clot forms. Each laceration results in an area of infection and inflammation.

(B) Constant movement of the worms over the inflamed intestine adds to the irritation.

(C) Severe, and sometimes rapid, loss of condition and accompanying anemia are usual symptoms. Diagnosis is confirmed by finding strongyles in the intestine upon autopsy of typical specimens.

(3) TREATMENT. Treatment is not satisfactory. One-half CC doses of tetrachlorethylene may be tried.

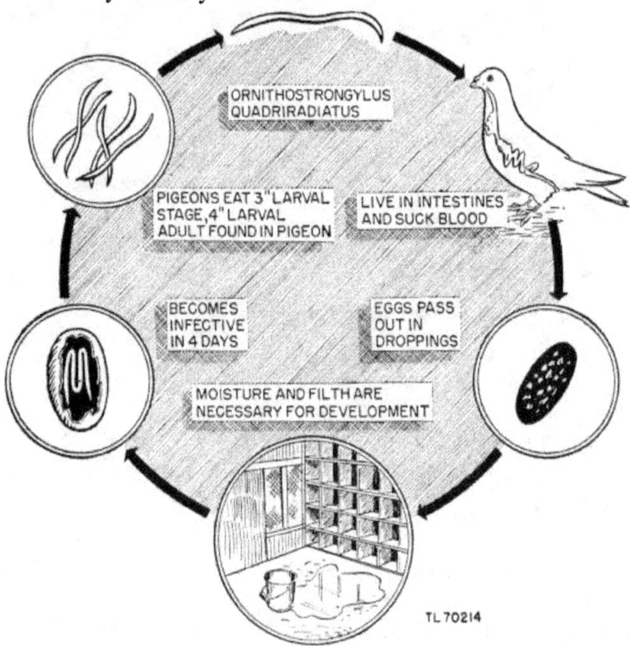

FIGURE 45. LIFE CYCLE OF PIGEON STRONGYLE.

(4) PREVENTION. The same methods prescribed for ascarids apply to strongyles.

C. Other round worms attacking pigeons are numerous, but only capillary worms will be discussed here. These are very thin, hair-like worms sometimes found in the digestive tract of pigeons from the crop down through the intestine. Their life cycle is direct. No satisfactory drug has been found to rid pigeons of this worm. Fortunately, their life cycle is similar to that of ascarids, and the same preventive measures are effective.

D. Tape worms, which are occasionally seen in pigeons, acquire a length of 6 to 8 inches.

(1) LIFE CYCLE. Tape worms have what is called an indirect life cycle, that is they must pass through at least two different species to complete it (**fig. 46**).

(A) Adult tape worms are found in the small intestine. Their bodies are made up of a head and segments. The head is essentially an anchor that fastens the worm to the intestine of the bird. The body segments form at the head and mature as they grow further from the head.

(B) Each segment contains both male and female sex organs and, as it matures, becomes virtually a packet of tape worm eggs.

(C) Segments break off and pass out in the feces.

(D) The tape worm's eggs are then eaten by a snail, slug, beetle, or other insect which becomes the "intermediate host." Here the tape worm undergoes a certain amount of development.

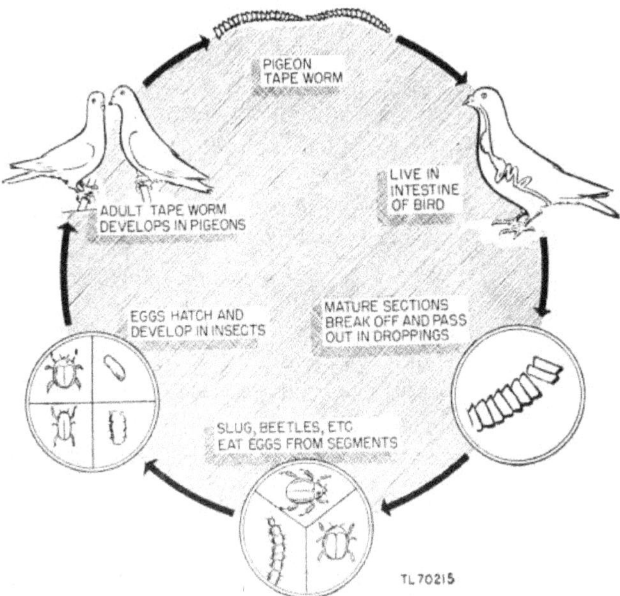

FIGURE 46. LIFE CYCLE OF PIGEON TAPE WORM.

(E) If the intermediate host is eaten by a pigeon, the young tape worm attaches itself to the bird's intestine and soon grows to maturity.

(2) DIAGNOSIS. Tape worms harm the host by injuring the intestine at the point where they bury their heads, by absorbing food, and by giving off antenzymes.

(3) TREATMENT. Unsatisfactory.

(4) PREVENTION. (A) Pigeons must be well-cared-for and fed so that they will not care to eat the intermediate hosts.

(B) The method of prevention prescribed for ascarids is also applicable for tape worms.

55. Treatment of Injuries

A. Cuts and wounds. Pigeons have marvelous powers of healing their own tissues, perhaps because of their high body temperature and rapid rate of body processes. The following are aids to healing.

(1) Clean solid or contaminated wounds with boric acid solution or some very mild antiseptic. Strong disinfectants burn the exposed tissues and delay wound healing.

(2) Stitch or suture large tears in the skin to make them relatively smaller. Avoid placing suture in such a way that a pocket is formed for this often results in an abscess formation. Use white silk or cotton thread.

(3) Remove excessively rough edges or hanging flaps of skin with sharp scissors.

B. Fractures. (1) Broken bones in the extremities of the legs usually respond readily to treatment; those involving the large bones present a more complicated problem.

(2) The type of fracture governs the seriousness of the injury.

(A) SIMPLE fractures are those in which there is no break in the skin in the region of the fracture.

(B) COMPOUND fractures are those in which there is a break in the skin over the bone injury.

(C) PARTIAL fractures are those in which the bone is cracked but not completely separated.

(D) COMPLETE fractures are those in which there is actual separation of the parts of bone.

(E) COMMINUTED fractures are those in which the bone is splintered or fragmented.

(3) Treatment of fractures is quite simple: bring broken parts into contact and immobilize them to avoid movement which might injure delicate healing tissues.

(A) Since bones heal in whatever position they are placed, it is necessary to splint the limb in as nearly normal a position as possible.

(B) Take care that the splint does not interfere with healing.

1. Do not bandage splint too tightly. The bandage must be snug to avoid movement of the parts, however, if it is too tight, the blood supply will be cut off and the limb will die. Splints applied before the injured limb has swollen must be closely observed for several hours, or until the swelling has reached its maximum so that circulation is not impeded.

2. Pad limb with cotton or gauze to protect it from the hard surfaces of the splint.

3. Dust powdered boric acid on the region of the fracture, particularly if the fracture is compound.

(C) Splints may be easily and satisfactorily fashioned from pieces of pliable tin. Cut and bend to fit contour of limb in normal resting position (**fig. 47**). Splints for fractures in the shank should extend down along the shank on one side, then bend to form a loop down around the foot and back up the opposite side of the limb. In a short time the bird learns that it can step on the limb without pain because the weight falls on the loop of the splint rather than on the foot.

(D) Splints should be left in place for 3 weeks before removing. Healing, if successful, will be sufficient to permit removal of splint at this time.

C. Torn crops. These may be successfully sutured if the edges are turned in so that the outside surfaces, not the lining, of the crop come in contact. The skin may then be sutured to help support the crop.

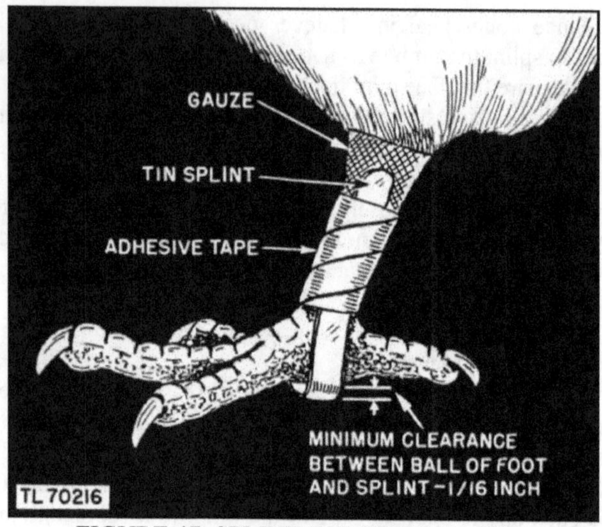

FIGURE 47. SPLINT FOR BROKEN LEG.

56. Medicines

The following items of medical supplies and equipment, in the quantities listed in existing instructions, should meet normal requirements.

33775	Needle, eye, size 4, 3/8-circle, 6-in.
36624	Cotton thread, No. 80, 150 yds.
77110	Basin, hand.
77410	Capsule, size 00, gelatin, 100.
77600	Cork, No. 2, ½ × 3/8 in., 100.
77950	Dropper, medicine.
78090	Graduate, 10-CC, glass.
79460	Vial, 1-oz., with screw cap.
91110	Iodine, 15 GR, and Potassium; iodide, 22.5-GR, USP, 10 tubes.

☆ U. S. Government Printing Office: 1945—621966